Small Company, Big Crisis is packed full of usefu[...] how to prepare for, get through and come out the other end of a crisis in business. I love the attention to detail on what we, as business owners need to do, and especially the sections on risk management and creating a cash reserve, the latter so often the reason that businesses don't survive a crisis.

— *Amanda Fisher aka The Cash Flow Queen*
— *Author and Financial Educator.*

Successfully managing risk normally comes from experience (and a dollop of luck). Business owners that had been through the Global Financial Crisis, or other downturns, were more able to navigate the recent pandemic. Bronwyn Reid selflessly shares her experience, drawing on plenty of global examples, to help you the business owner, make sure you are as well prepared as possible to deal with the inevitable bumps in the road, big or small, on your way to success. Just remember to keep your sense of humour ...

— *Callum Laing, CEO MBH Corporation PLC.*

This book is an excellent synopsis of what is happening in the world of business today. It gives business owners some excellent ideas about how to navigate the future of business, especially after Covid is history. A definite read for both small and large business people.

— *Ian Dainty, CEO Maximize Business Marketing.*

If you are in business and in particular a small business this book is one you need to grab with both hands and devour! A well -structured gold mine of 'How-To's', tips, and tactics that every business owner should know and have in their arsenal.

Easy to read, this book will enable your business to prepare for and come through the other side of pretty much any crisis in good shape.

— *Geoff Hetherington, The Profitability Coach,*
Founder Elite Business Institute.

From my experience, working with business owners around the world, very few plan for the inevitable crisis that they have to deal with. The result is business failure. At long last a very smart and practical book has been written to help business owners start to not only navigate their way through any kind of crisis but also to learn from the crisis they face and to become much stronger. Small Company, Big Crisis is an essential read for every single business owner.

— Andrew Griffiths, International Bestselling Author,
Global Speaker, Entrepreneurial Futurist.

Bronwyn Reid

SMALL COMPANY
BIG
CRISIS

How to prepare for,
respond to, and recover
from a business crisis

ind*i.e.* —
experts
IN OTHER WORDS

First published 2021 by Bronwyn Reid

Produced by Indie Experts
indieexperts.com.au

Copyright © Bronwyn Reid 2021

Cover design by Daniela Catucci
Edited by Samantha Sainsbury
Illustrations by Bronwyn Reid
Typeset in 12/16.5 pt Adobe Garamond Pro by Post Pre-press Group, Brisbane

A catalogue record for this
book is available from the
National Library of Australia

NATIONAL
LIBRARY
OF AUSTRALIA

ISBN 978-0-6451277-0-6 (pbk)
ISBN 978-0-6451277-1-3 (epub)
ISBN 978-0-6451277-2-0 (kindle)

Disclaimer:
Any information in the book is purely the opinion of the author based on her personal experience and should not be taken as business or legal advice. All material is provided for educational purposes only. We recommend to always seek the advice of a qualified professional before making any decision regarding personal and business needs.

To my family. Everything is for you. And the dogs.

CONTENTS

Foreword
by Kate Carnell AO

The year that was 2020 was the toughest in living memory for many Australian small businesses.

A catastrophic bushfire season, closely followed by a global pandemic that forced thousands of small businesses to close their doors and many more impacted by restricted trade.

Economic activity dived to levels not seen since the Great Depression and although the recession was short-lived, it was sharp and punishing for the small business sector.

Overall small businesses faced these extraordinary challenges with admirable courage. Many have proven to be resilient, while others have been decimated.

2020 was tumultuous, but it also delivered some important lessons for small businesses – even if they were learned the hard way.

As Small Company Big Crisis rightly points out – economic downturns do happen. Planning for them could change the outcome markedly.

Drawing on research from the University of Queensland, this book identifies the critical success factors to ensure your business is resilient – among them are adaptiveness and proactiveness.

A small business' ability to adapt and react quickly to changes were more likely to survive an economic upheaval. According to the Australian Bureau of Statistics, 40% of Australian small businesses changed the way they provided products and services at the peak of the COVID crisis.

Digitisation was key to this. We know many small businesses made decades worth of change in the space of a few months in 2020. In fact, having a digital presence and e-commerce capabilities is now essential. Online shopping has been steadily increasing over the years, but there was significant growth in 2020. In December 2020, online sales rose by more than 70% compared to the same period in 2019. MYOB data suggests SMEs with advanced levels of digital engagement are 50% more likely to grow revenue and earn 60% more revenue per employee.

Proactive business owners, vigilant about the opportunities and threats in the environment, have faired better than others. As this book highlights, being prepared for what needs to happen within the business when disaster strikes, is critical. This means having a risk management strategy in place. It means leaning on your trusted, accredited advisors to help map out a path and consider the best and worst scenarios before they happen.

Another standout message I have taken from reading Small Company Big Crisis, is the importance of protecting your reputation by behaving ethically – especially during a crisis. In times of trouble, it's critical to resist any temptation to take advantage of the situation in a manner that comes at the expense of others. It's absolutely true that your actions in a crisis will be remembered by your customers and your community. A short-term gain is not worth the long-term pain.

Above all, Small Company Big Crisis, offers timely and relevant tips for small business owners who want to control the future of their business.

The events of 2020 have taken a toll, but I have been inspired by the courage and agility of the Australian small business community. Their fighting spirit will be what helps them get to the other side of this crisis and the inevitable downturns to come.

Introduction

The year 2020 started with such high hopes. At least, it did for me. At the end of January, I fulfilled a lifelong dream of visiting Antarctica. I departed from Brisbane on 24 January with my long-time friend Pat. By the time we boarded our ship *Expedition* in Ushuaia on 30 January, there were already mumblings about a virus affecting people in China, and the province of Wuhan had moved into lockdown.

From there, things went downhill.

On 25 January, Australia confirmed its first case.

On 7 February, Li Wenliang, one of the eight whistleblower doctors in Wuhan who alerted the world to the new virus, died from the coronavirus.

Onboard *Expedition*, we had a daily, printed, one-page newsletter with selected stories from around the globe, which served as our only source of news from the outside world. From there, we learned about Li Wenliang and received snippets of coronavirus news from many countries.[1]

By the time we disembarked back in Ushuaia on 12 February, things were really starting to fall apart. I flew home to Australia

---

1   Bizarrely, Barnaby Joyce's tilt for another go at the National Party leadership on 4 February also made the *Expedition* newsletter. The Australians on board were not amused.

on 14 February via Buenos Aires and Santiago, while my friend continued on her adventures to Easter Island and the Galapagos. By the time she arrived back in Australia, Pat was obliged to do 14 days of self-quarantine at home. Airports and entire countries were closing behind her.

On 11 March, the World Health Organisation declared the COVID-19 outbreak a pandemic.

All of a sudden, the world realised that it was facing a monster – one that would claim millions of lives, cause business to shut down, stock markets (and therefore wealth) to tank, GDP to plummet, and unemployment to skyrocket. The Australian Government suddenly announced hundreds of millions of dollars of stimulus packages to replace the private spending that had vanished in just a few short weeks.

Thus began 2020 with the biggest bust in a century.

This book draws on my experience of crises over many years in business with my husband, Ian.

Our environmental consultancy, 4T Consultants, has many mining companies as clients. We help them to comply with their statutory requirements and community expectations in environmental performance.

In 2012–2013, the Australian resources boom turned into a mining bust, and we lost two-thirds of our revenue very, very rapidly. We lost at least six contracts (I stopped counting) in quick succession. All of those contracts were fully resourced with people, vehicles and equipment. We got one phone call after the another saying: "Sorry, the project's cancelled." Terrifying stuff.

And then in early 2020, that same thing happened to thousands of other Australian small-businesses owners. First with the bushfires, and then with COVID-19.

Facing such extraordinary crises is horrifying and shocking. You might have experienced a similar crisis yourself already or you may be looking to future-proof your venture against such seismic business upheaval. Whatever your circumstances, the purpose of this book is to help you confront the inevitable, protect your business and maybe even grow stronger as a result of the disaster.

Crises don't just come in the form of natural disasters, economic downturns and pandemics. A death, a divorce, fraud, a computer hack ... All these events, and many, many more can fatally derail a business.

What would you do if a crisis struck tomorrow? How would you react? Would you be like a rabbit in the headlights, frozen in fear and bewilderment, not knowing what to do?

I'm sure you will be familiar with the fight or flight response to a feared stimulus. The fight or flight response is a primitive and powerful survival reaction. Imagine a spider were to suddenly fall from the ceiling onto you as you read this. You have two options: get the spider off you, or get away from it as quickly as possible.

What many of us don't know, however, is that there is a third approach when we come across a dangerous scenario – freeze. The least adaptive of the three possible reactions, our brains sometimes choose to freeze when we are completely overwhelmed with fear. We become paralysed.

Rabbits (and kangaroos and deer ...) haven't figured out that playing dead isn't such a good thing to do when a vehicle is bearing down on them, but you can understand why they freeze. They are hoping that the threat will go away.

And that's exactly the risk we face as business owners when we encounter an economic threat such as the coronavirus pandemic, or a flood, or fire, or family crisis. Our brains freeze, we play dead, and we hope that the bad thing will go away.

In our case, we did survive the resources downturn as an environmental business. We were bruised and battered, but we are still here to tell the tale. That experience, plus the stock market booms and busts that we have managed to survive, (1987, 2000–2001, 2008), as well as two major natural disasters in 2008 and 2011, have taught us a couple of things about surviving economic threats.

I hope that some of the lessons we learned can help other small-business owners, both as business owners and as individuals. In fact, the relevance of this book is not limited to business owners at all. There are lessons that we can all take to heart and use in difficult situations.

This book is a collection of my thoughts and experiences in understanding and getting through a business crisis without freezing, and then being run over, like the rabbit in the headlights. In this book, I'll explore the history of booms and busts and the practical actions you can put in place today to ensure your business weathers the storm. Finally, I'll cast an eye to the future and the opportunities that might develop in the wake of a crisis, and the ways we can all seek to do business better.

Each crisis will pass, but we can be sure that another will follow. Your business doesn't need to fall victim to unforeseen circumstances. With some sensible forward planning, you can feel confident in your ability to make it to the light at the end of the proverbial tunnel.

Chapter 1
The Anatomy of Booms and Busts

Economic booms are periods when the prices of some underlying assets increase, slowly at first, then rapidly, then exponentially. The asset concerned may be house prices, coal, tulip bulbs (more on this shortly), sugar, oil, share prices, or anything else that can have a price ascribed to it. Share-price booms are familiar to most of us. Many readers will recall the Tech Boom, or Dot Com Bubble, of the late 1990s–early 2000s, so I will use that as an example.

Between 1995 and March 2000, the US stock market index of technology stocks (the Nasdaq Composite Index) increased by 400 percent. The stock market is an indicator of economic health. If investors think that the economy is healthy and companies will be profitable, they will invest in a company's shares and cause the share price to increase. If investors see trouble ahead, the opposite occurs. Thus, the share market is a "leading indicator" of economic conditions to come.

Even though small, private companies like mine are not represented in the main stock-market indices, their fortunes also ride on the outlook of stock-market investors. We sell our goods and services to the big companies and also buy from them. Some of our customers are employed by those big companies. If investors are pessimistic, they won't be spending money.

It's all a big, tangled, interwoven economic web.

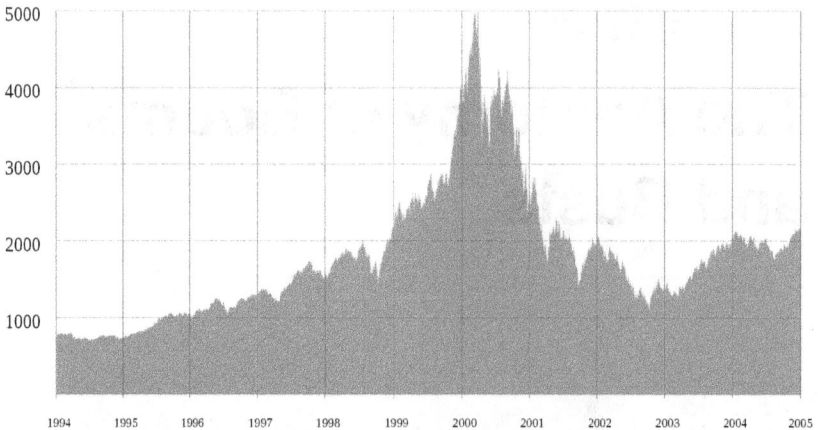

Graph: The shape of a boom and bust: The US Nasdaq Composite Index that measures the value of technology shares increased by 400 percent between 1995 and 2000. Source: https://commons.wikimedia.org/w/index.php?curid=3189816

During the latter stages of the Tech Boom, any company that had a vague connection to anything remotely related to the internet became a market darling. The fact that many of these hopefuls had no product and no market, and absolutely no hope of achieving either, did not prevent them from reaching astronomical prices. Everyone, it seemed, was in on the act, and the proverbial shoe-shine boy[2] would be able to tell you about "the next big thing".

---

2   There is a story that Joe Kennedy, the millionaire investor and father of the future President John F. Kennedy, was once given a tip to buy a certain stock while having his shoes shined. Supposedly, Kennedy sold out of his stocks, remarking that "If shoe-shine boys are giving stock tips, then it's time to get out of the market."

Such was the exuberance of the market about all things technology-related, that on 10 January 2000, America Online (AOL), an internet-subscription provider, announced a merger with Time Warner, a cable-television company. The merger, worth USD$180 billion, was the largest ever recorded.

At the height of this boom/bubble, a familiar phrase could be seen in multiple newspapers, stockbrokers' research reports and business commentary. The phrase was "this time it's different". This simple phrase allowed analysts, pundits and investors to dispense with all the traditional market-valuation tools such as discounted cashflow analysis, and even whether the company had a product to sell.

Then came the bust.

The rot set in during the first weeks of March 2000. The high point occurred on 10 March 2000 and the decline started from there but proceeded rapidly. The bubble had burst. By October 2002, the low point, the Nasdaq Composite Index had fallen 78 percent from the peak. All the gains were gone. That much-talked-about merger between AOL and Time Warner wiped out USD$99 billion of shareholder wealth. Overall, some USD$7 trillion of market value was destroyed. Not one of corporate America's shining moments.

This time it's different? Actually, it's never different …

This potted history of the Tech Boom (or the Tech Wreck as it became known) encapsulates the trajectory of all booms and busts. They are all the same general shape and evoke the same psychology in their unfolding phases as they play out. All of them. Up by the stairs, down by the elevator.

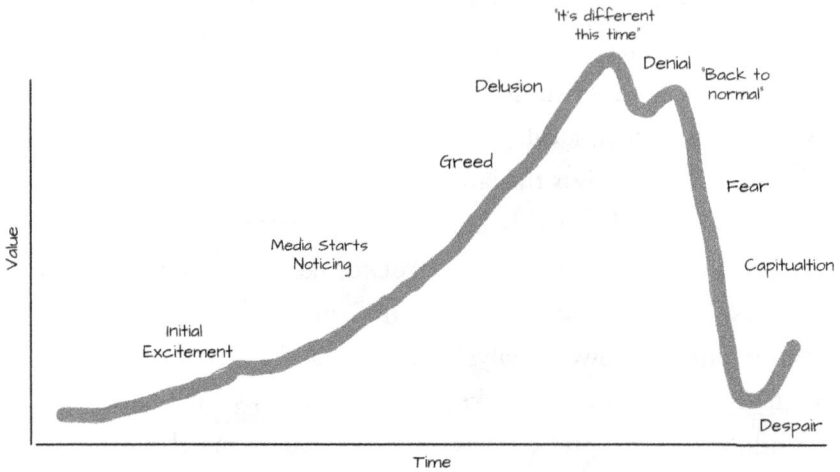

The boom–bust cycle unfolds in six phases.

The beginning. There will be a precursor to the boom, usually something is invented or happens that creates a shift. In the case of the Dot Com Bubble, the precursor was the creation of the World Wide Web in 1993. The leaders and technology early adopters picked it up and started tinkering.

The awakening. Eventually, the media starts to notice that something is happening. At this point, the speed of the boom begins to accelerate.

The boom. As word spreads, more and more people, including the proverbial shoe-shine boy, want to have a piece of the action, the easy money. The price escalation accelerates, and any vestige of reason is dispensed with. Eventually, the boom reaches the "this time it's different" point, and the end is nigh. Interestingly, in this final phase, there will be mega-mergers such as the AOL–Time Warner one referred to earlier.

In the lead-up to the next great boom and bust, the Global Financial Crisis, mega-miner BHP pursued its rival Rio Tinto. When the deal was called off in the face of a potential global meltdown of the financial system, Rio Tinto's shares fell 37 percent. Again, millions of dollars of shareholder wealth were destroyed.

You could refer to this end phase as the "when elephants dance" phase.

The tipping point. There is no way of telling what the final straw will be. It may be a single cause, or an accumulation of factors. Put simply, nobody rings a bell at the top. It is up to each of us to try to read the tea leaves in the run up to the top and prepare for the inevitable without a timeframe.

The initial drop is always followed by a bounce. Bargain hunters scavenge for value and bid up prices. Almost everyone else is relieved. "Phew! We survived that scare, but now everything is back to normal ..." Those who study markets now become active sellers, pushing prices back into decline.

Fear and selling. As the selling resumes, all sorts of emotions take hold. Denial is one – it's all going to be ok. Fear is another, and fear leads to denial. Wealth is impacted. People feel less wealthy and therefore spend less. Eventually, the wealth-squeeze forces those who joined the party late to exit and crystallise their losses. The hold-outs stay until the end, until they too capitulate, exhausted from the emotional and financial losses they have endured.

Despair, and a new beginning. At this stage, there is nothing good. Newspapers and commentators expound gloom. Despair has taken hold. But at the same time, the foundations for a new beginning have been laid. Somewhere, someone has invented or done something that will eventually spark the next cycle. Our challenge is to continually scan the horizon for that thing and try to be one of the leaders into the next boom.

The 2019–2020 boom

The boom of 2019–2020 was not as pronounced as some previous ones, for example the Dot Com Boom I have described, and the resources boom of the late 2000s. It certainly wasn't the same here in Australia as it was in the USA, where Donald Trump had business in a frenzy – rightly or wrongly. Massive stock buy-backs by American companies (where they use their money to buy their own shares instead of investing in projects) had pushed share prices higher.[3] Australia's economy was showing signs of weakness. In fact, Australia had already dipped into a per-capita recession[4] in March 2019, a full 12 months before COVID-19 struck.

So while the classic shape of the boom and bust graph may have been muted and the shark feeding frenzy that usually accompanies market tops wasn't completely in-your-face, there were clear caution signs.[5, 6]

Everything old is new again

In a book called *Extraordinary Popular Delusions and the Madness of Crowds,* psychologist Charles Mackay describes the anatomy of several booms and busts of bygone eras. Mackay's book was first published in 1841, which goes to show that these cycles are by no means a new phenomenon.

In the 1630s, Tulip Mania swept through Holland. Tulip bulbs (yes, the flowers) became the subject of a mad rush. Everyone suddenly, absolutely, had to own tulip bulbs, and their price went sky-high. One bulb was purchased for 4600 florins, a new carriage,

---

3   When a company buys its own shares, there are fewer shares available for other investors to buy. Because the assets and the earnings of the company overall are still the same, the price per share increases.

4   Economists call a recession when total real gross national product declines for two consecutive quarters. A per-capita recession is when the GDP per person declines for two consecutive quarters.

5   "Global recession a serious danger in 2020, says UN" https://www.theguardian.com/business/2019/sep/25/global-recession-a-serious-danger-in-2020-says-un

6   "Is there a recession coming? Keep an eye on these key indicators" https://www.cnbc.com/2019/09/30/is-there-a-recession-coming-keep-an-eye-on-these-key-indicators.html

two grey horses and a complete set of harnesses. Now, it is exceedingly difficult to equate 4600 florins in the 1600s to dollars now, but I did find one genealogy site that used inflation and CPI research, exchange rates and purchasing power to give an exchange-rate figure of about 60. If this is correct, somebody purchased a tulip bulb for USD$27,600,000 – plus the horses, the carriage and the harness. I guess it seemed like a good idea at the time …

And as with the tulip boom, every single time the trigger that causes the bust is an unknown. In 2020, a left-field event – a highly contagious virus with no vaccine – brought the world economy and the market to its knees.

Unfortunately, these booms and busts are inevitable. Most probably, you will experience a few of them in your lifetime. And yet, we never seem to be prepared. We're always surprised. In the aftermath of each bust, we declare that we will learn from the experience and we vow that we won't make the same mistakes next time. In the 2012–2013 resources-industry bust, I spoke to innumerable business owners who swore blind that next time they wouldn't fall for the hype and encouragement (and bullying) of the mining industry. Maybe they won't, but there will be a whole new crop of business owners who will.

Booms and busts are inevitable. And yet we never seem to be prepared.

When the world faces a massive bust, businesses across the board are impacted in myriad ways. While the busts are inevitable, the devastation left in their wake is not. I would love to help you protect your business from major damage by using my experience to help you survive when experiencing your big bust.

Chapter 2
Being a Resilient Business

Going into 2020, COVID-19, and the subsequent economic down-turn, there were hundreds of thousands of business owners who did not remember the last time Australia had experienced a recession. It was 30 years previously in 1990–1991. The unemployment rate rose to 10.8 percent, business interest rates hovered around 20 percent, several financial institutions failed, and some high-flying entrepreneurs fell into bankruptcy. *Some of them ended up in jail.*

Those of us who survived that recession carry the scars from that time, and hopefully learned some lessons. There will be younger entrepreneurs reading this, however, who have never experienced a recession, or know what it is to run a business when the world turns against you. Yes, we had the Global Financial Crisis in 2008, but Australia as a whole managed to escape relatively unscathed (in comparison to other countries) from that mess.

How did we manage that? Australia has two economies: the resources economy and the general economy. During the Global Financial Crisis, the resources economy was booming, so much so that it managed to prevent the overall national economy from slipping into recession. Many businesses outside the resources industry, however, felt the full force of the financial implosion that was the GFC.

With this being said, there are also many businesses that survived the recession 30 years ago. Similarly, there are businesses that emerged from the wreckage of the recent mining boom and bust. And there will be businesses that survive the COVID-19 pandemic.

These are the **resilient** ones.

What does "resilience" mean?

Put the word "resilience" into any internet search engine and you will come up with literally millions of results – about 235,000,000 the day I tried it.

To pick one definition, the Oxford Dictionary states that resilience is:

"the capacity to recover quickly from difficulties; toughness".

The UQ Business School (more about this soon) states that:

"Organisational resilience [is] the capacity to respond, adapt and transform in response to changes in the business environment."

In psychology, resilience includes the possibility of personal growth to the definition:

"Becoming more resilient not only helps you get through difficult circumstances, it also empowers you to grow and even improve your life along the way."[7]

---

7   American Psychological Association https://www.apa.org/topics/resilience

What does resilience mean for your business?

While the general definition of resilience is quite clear, you need to think clearly about what resilience means to you and your business. In the face of a crisis or a bust, what outcome would represent resilience for your business?

- Does it mean that your business survives intact, even though it may be much smaller?
- Does it mean that you extract yourself and your family from the business with sufficient funds to start again?
- Does it mean that you will have the will and the energy to rebuild if all is lost?

Your own personal definition of resilience will determine how you prepare for and cope with adverse events, such as booms and busts.

So before you read any further, please give this question of what resilience means for your business some consideration, as it will colour how you read and interpret the remainder of what I have written.

To help you answer the question, I have gathered some resources on my website at **bronwynreid.com.au/resources**.

Why do some businesses thrive while others don't?

These are the big questions. Why do some businesses make it to the other side of the despair phase of a bust, ready to ride the recovery curve upwards?

After the resources bust, the University of Queensland conducted a study of small business resilience.[8] The goal of this

---

8   https://natural-gas.centre.uq.edu.au/article/2016/09/key-capabilities-helping-small-businesses-survive-end-resource-boom.

study was to discover any common characteristics of businesses that survived. The results of the study reflect my own experience, and are equally applicable to any small business, in any area, in any industry.

The UQ Four Critical Success Factors

According to the UQ study, there are **four success factors** that determine the resilience of a business and whether a business dies, survives or thrives when hit by a major economic upheaval:

- adaptiveness
- proactiveness
- connectedness
- slack.

Adaptiveness

Adaptiveness means being able to **react quickly** to changes. You need to be able to turn your business on a dime, reallocate resources, or even change the resources you use to retain market share and position. Adaptive businesses are highly focussed on **customer satisfaction**. There were many, many examples of this during COVID-19, most notably the way we all adapted to using Zoom and other technology solutions. These tools allowed many to keep working while staying at home, as well as attending regular meetings and virtual conferences. I even MC'd my first ever completely online conference. That was an interesting experience, and the technology only failed once!

There were some excellent, innovative and even amusing examples of adaptive businesses that cropped up during COVID-19. So many, in fact, that a website (covidinnovations.com) was born to list them all.

For instance, an acclaimed music school began teaching via video links. The Major Player Music School is based in Rockhampton, Queensland. Like all music (and non-music) schools, their face-to-face lessons came to a shuddering halt during the COVID-19 lockdowns. Owners Bernadette Gorman and Steve Nicholls adapted immediately, recruiting the parent of one of their students to get the technology sorted. Rockhampton is a regional Queensland city, and Major Player's students come from far and wide. The new online system created a wonderful outcome in making music accessible to children who otherwise would never have the opportunity to know the joys of musicianship.

"It's not the strongest species that survives, nor the most intelligent, but the one most responsive to change."
Charles Darwin

Another of my favourites is a Melbourne bakery whose owners stared down the pandemic lockdown with style. They began producing "bake at home" kits. For just $10, you could get everything you needed to bake your own delicious sourdough at home. They even included a little extra starter in case you wanted to make even more sourdough. Tivoli Bakery began selling their kits way back in March 2020, right at the beginning of the lockdown era. Many others cottoned on later, but Tivoli was certainly amongst the leaders.[9]

It's a well-worn analogy, but Mr Charles Darwin said it best a long time ago: "It's not the strongest species that survives, nor the most intelligent, but the one most responsive to change."

9   https://www.instagram.com/p/B9z0K8dJ-Fq/

Proactiveness

The proactive business owner is constantly on the lookout for opportunities and threats in the environment.

To be proactive you must be hyper-vigilant about:

- what's happening around you,
- what's happening in your industry, and
- what's happening in the economy.

Be prepared to introduce new products or services rapidly, or even change the entire organisational structure when necessary. The proactive business owner is committed to both their own self-development and development of their staff.

Take Susan Bryant, for example. Aside from being one of my closest friends, she is a shining example of what a proactive business looks like. She also happens to be a financial advisor who has accumulated a lifetime of wisdom on negotiating the vagaries of financial markets.[10]

After the 2008 Global Financial Crisis, Susan decided that there must be a better way. Having to have "the conversation" with clients one more time was just too much. So, as the truly proactive business owner will do, she set about researching and further educating herself. She knew that there would be another economic downturn, and she simply didn't want her clients to suffer again.

As a result, Susan approaches investing from a different angle. All the usual financial spruikers concentrate on telling you about returns – how their investments will earn you the biggest return. Anything about risk is in size six font on the back page.

Susan is focussed on the risk side of the coin. She starts with her clients' financial goals and needs. She then figures out what her

---

10   https://www.seedsofadvice.com/

client will need to get there without taking on the risk that we have witnessed in the past. The risk (volatility, or those big ups and downs you see on the tv news) is the focus point – not just aiming for the big returns.

As a result, Susan's clients came through the coronavirus market gyrations with their investments largely intact or even positive.

Connectedness

To me, connectedness is a subset of proactiveness. The connected business owner will cultivate and keep an active network of suppliers, advisers, customers, peers and strategic partners who will help to keep tabs on what is happening in the industry and community. In addition, these networks will give you access to other market segments or industries.

How do you become and remain connected as a business owner? In my book, *Small Company, Big Business,* there is an entire chapter on how your "external team" can be an invaluable source of market intelligence and information. Your external team consists of your accountant, lawyer, insurance broker, business mentor – all those professionals you hire to give you the advice you need to both comply with the law and run a successful business.

Apart from your external team, there are professional associations, business groups, meet-ups, LinkedIn, Facebook groups, and even the social setting of a bar. Your connectedness is only limited by your willingness and imagination!

Slack

"Slack" is the ability to source **additional resources** (equipment, skilled staff, finance) to meet additional demand, or to take advantage of opportunities as they present themselves. In a crisis, having additional resources available may or may not be useful, depending on how they can be used within our limitations. Holding on to slack resources is the direct antithesis to the "Cut Early and Cut Hard" dictum I will discuss later in Chapter 4.

For our environmental consultancy, 4T Consultants, having some slack during the coronavirus pandemic proved to be highly valuable. Once the state borders closed, some of our competitors' personnel were not able to come to Queensland to perform their work. As a local company, we picked up the slack (pardon the pun).

These four factors of success give you an excellent sense of what makes a business truly resilient. But there are more elements to consider to bust-proof your business. I have researched several free questionnaires available that will help you understand how resilient you are. The links to these questionnaires can be accessed from the Small Company, Big Crisis page on my website bronwynreid.com.au.

Chapter 3

The Seven-Question Framework for a Resilient Business

While the UQ list is an excellent guide, and is based on rigorous research, I have a few factors of my own that come from my own (expensive) experience.

In this chapter, I want to pose 7 questions that will enable you to build a resilient business.

QUESTION 1: Do you have a Risk Management Strategy?

There is a saying that the only sure things are death and taxes. I would add the inevitability of booms and busts, and other manifestations of business crises. And as you survive one crisis, you can be sure that another one will be along in the future. Natural disasters have always been a part of business life in Australia, but the frequency and severity of extreme weather events is increasing as climate change takes effect. Starting in 2020, we had a pandemic in the mix.

What I'm talking about is risk. Every business should have a basic Risk Management Plan in place. What should we do to prepare ourselves, our teams and our businesses for things that can go wrong?

Because these hazardous events and crises will always occur, it is important that small-business owners take the time to think about the hazards they face and make some plans about what to do if the worst happens.

Hazards aren't only limited to nature and the economy, however. In late 2019, I took an unplanned ride in an ambulance from Brisbane Airport to the Royal Brisbane Hospital. I was already buckled into my seat on the plane when I began to feel extremely unwell. The crew members noticed and called for an ambulance.

Fortunately, I was ok, and I was back home within a few days. That being said, the experience of being very ill on an aeroplane – luckily before it took off – was quite frightening. All sorts of things were running through my mind, and amongst those things were our businesses.

What if something bad was happening with my health? What if I couldn't continue to be an active director? Would the plans I have in place be sufficient?

It's a grim subject, I know, but a part of your obligations as a small-business owner is considering what happens if you are no longer able to be the driving force. Are your insurances in place and adequate? Are your systems documented so that someone else could step in? There is so much to consider, and you will probably need some expert guidance. (There's that external team again that I keep talking about.)

If risk management is so helpful, why doesn't everyone do it?

We all know logically that we need to have risk-management proce-
dures in place for our business. So why don't we?

Over my years of working with small business, I have come
across a few reasons business owners avoid investing time and money
into risk management.

- Business owners are optimists by nature. They will always look
  on the upside for possible business outcomes.
- Business owners already have a higher tolerance of risk than
  their corporate colleagues. Otherwise they wouldn't be in business in the first place.
- "I've got too much work to do running the business. I don't
  have time to deal with that stuff."
- "It won't happen to me."
- "It's just a tick and flick exercise anyway. Nobody takes any real
  notice of it."

Do any of these sound familiar? Be honest … If so, you definitely
need to reassess your attitude towards business risk. Read on!

Risk management

Risk management doesn't have to be a huge, complex process, but
we need to contemplate and develop a plan that takes into account
the following.

1. Identifying things that could go wrong.
2. What would happen if they did go wrong?
3. How we can help prevent those things from happening.
4. What to do if the worst did happen.

Your risk identification won't be spot-on all the time (I certainly didn't have a global pandemic in our Risk Management Plan), but some preparation is infinitely better than none, and a small amount of time spent now can save a world of pain later. Also, if you have done your preparatory thinking, it's not too hard to adapt your plan to a new crisis that sneaks up on you.

A small amount of time spent now can save
a world of pain later.

Having a Risk Management Plan allowed our environmental consultancy, 4T Consultants, to go through a flood in January 2011, with minimal damage and disruption, and be back up and operating within 48 hours. As a result of a previous flood in 2008 (that fortunately didn't reach our home or office), we were aware of the danger levels as the floodwaters rose. River levels are recorded by automatic monitoring stations up and down the river. When the river levels reached those danger points upstream of our home and office, the plan swung into action. Everything was methodically packed up and moved out of harm's way. Within 48 hours of the water receding, we were able to continue providing service to our clients – with one computer on a plastic table.

I am not in any way suggesting that the floods we went through were anything like the severity of what our fellow Australians went through in the 2019–2020 bushfires, or the forced closures due to COVID-19. We had five days to wait for the water to come down, and water follows a pretty predictable course. However, having a flood plan in our own business meant that everyone knew what to do and when. We knew that when the water level rose to a certain level at a certain station, we were going to act.

Identifying things that could go wrong and what would happen

Natural disasters are an obvious hazard, as in the case of floods, cyclones or fire but these aren't the only ones. If a key employee leaves, a computer system is hacked, or a key supplier disappears, a business can be crippled. Perhaps a family crisis hits. The incapacitation or death of a family member has been the end of many family businesses. The death of a loved one is enough to rob many of the will to continue the business as an ongoing concern.

Still, most small-business owners I have worked with are eternal optimists. They assure me that there are no risks to their business, and everything is under control. Hence, I find it useful to make a few suggestions and pose some questions to start them thinking.

Here is a list to start you thinking.

- **Natural disasters** such as fire, flood, cyclones and severe storms.
- **Personal health crisis.** You could suddenly fall ill.
- **Personal crises with family or friends.** Something could happen to a family member, or someone close to you.
- **Staff.** A key employee leaves, or fraudulent behaviour.
- **Information Technology**. You could be subject to a computer hack, or loss of data.
- **Technology**. Technology changes can render your product or service redundant. Video tapes were superseded by DVDs, which have been largely superseded by streaming services.
- **Market risk**. Economic cycles, competition, or changes in consumer tastes.
- **Customers**. Your biggest customer/s change to another supplier.
- **Suppliers**. Dependence upon a single or limited suppliers that disappear.
- **Pandemics**. This wasn't on my original list of risks, but it certainly is now.

This is by no means an exhaustive list, but it is a good place for small-business owners to start thinking about the specific risks that their business faces.

Risk-management tools

There are several simple tools that small-business owners can use to identify and manage risk. A brainstorming session can be the difference between surviving a left-field event and the business going under.

Here is a simple process to follow.

1. With your team, brainstorm and identify the things that could go wrong in your business.
2. What is the likelihood of these things happening?
3. If they do happen, what will the impact be?
4. Consult the Risk Matrix (see below) to identify the risk level.
5. Decide and document how you are going to manage this risk.

A brainstorming session can be the difference between surviving a left-field event and the business going under.

A simple example of a risk assessment is shown on the following page, and a template is available from my website[11, 12] As you can see, it doesn't have to be a massive document or a complex process. Of course, the more in-depth your risk assessments and risk-management plans are, the better prepared you will be.

---

11 A copy of these templates is available from my website bronwynreid.com.au
12 The Risk Matrix is widely used in risk management, but it does have limitations. More sophisticated tools are beyond the scope of this book.

But as I wrote earlier, some preparation is always better than none.

RISK	CHANCE OF IT HAPPENING	IMPACT IF IT HAPPENS	RISK LEVEL	HOW IT IS MANAGED
Loss of data or hacking	Rare	Major	High	Back-ups, IT Maintenance & Redundancy
Loss of key staff member	Occasional	Moderate	Medium	Documented Systems, Multi-skilling of staff
Fire	Low	Major	High	Data storage off site, Disaster recovery plan.

LIKELIHOOD	CONSEQUENCE				
	Insignificant	Minor	Moderate	Major	Catastrophic
ALMOST CERTAIN	High	High	Extreme	Extreme	Extreme
LIKELY	Medium	High	High	Extreme	Extreme
OCCASIONAL	Low	Medium	High	Extreme	Extreme
UNLIKELY	Low	Low	Medium	High	Extreme
RARE	Low	Low	Medium	High	High

And there is one thing that is 100 percent guaranteed. There will be another crisis to deal with sometime down the track.

QUESTION 2: Do you have a cash reserve?

In order to make your business resilient in the face of disaster, I recommend having a cash reserve. That little nest egg of emergency funding could make all the difference if the worst should occur.

Now, I know that putting aside cash is difficult. As I write this book, interest rates are virtually zero and are negative in some countries. But that doesn't mean you shouldn't at least try to accumulate some cash for a rainy day. The average small business has sufficient cash reserves for 27 days. (This figure is from 2015 research by JP Morgan Chase). We clearly saw what happens when cash stops flowing, or at least slows down, during the financial crisis, the mining downturn and, on a massive scale, during the 2020 COVID-19 pandemic.

Take the airline Virgin Australia, for example, which had long been operating with high levels of debt – $5 billion dollars of debt, to be exact. Once COVID-19 travel restrictions were implemented, cashflow virtually halted for the airline, and administrators were called in after the Federal Government refused an AU$1.4 billion loan. It sounds shocking, until you realise that Virgin Australia had reported a profit only once in the past decade, as well as borrowing an estimated $6 billion to bring the airline up to scratch to compete with QANTAS. With QANTAS dominating over 60 percent of the market, Virgin Australia struggled to gain enough scale to generate sufficient cashflow in order to alleviate their debt.

Come COVID-19, and without adequate cash reserves, Virgin Australia was backed into a corner. Their cashflow came to a standstill, and they did not have the revenue to keep their head above water. As a result, they entered voluntary administration, and were forced to stand down 8,000 of their 10,000 staff. Similar stories emerged across the globe.

The fear of mass business closures and the inevitable, terrible consequences of those closures is what forced governments worldwide into distributing vast amounts of cash as the pandemic unfolded. This cash allowed those businesses to continue paying their employees and stay solvent. Governments are very well aware of the consequences of running out of cash.[13]

A good idea is to keep your cash reserve in a completely separate bank account. Transfer small amounts from your regular cashflow. Accumulating a small amount regularly will not seem painful. In fact, you may not even notice that it's not there.

It was a cash reserve, built up over the good years, that was a major factor in our environmental company surviving to live another day when we were smashed by the resources-industry bust. There is a downside to be careful of when you have a good cash reserve though. The level of comfort you feel from knowing that cash is there to support your business may dull your instincts to "Cut Hard and Cut Early" as I suggest later in Chapter 4.

What's a good amount of cash to keep?

This is another one of those "how long is a piece of string" questions. But we can take a guide from financial gurus who recommend between three and six months of your regular expenses. But even that is not clear-cut. There are so many variables in business cash flows.

Seasonal businesses

For example, think of a farmer who grows one or two crops for sale every year. For the majority of the months in the year, cash flows out as the ground is prepared, seed planted, fertiliser is applied … Then, there are one or two big cash inflows when the crop has been

---

13　To understand how terrified governments are of running out of cash, watch the HBO documentary **Panic: The Untold Story of the 2008 Financial Crisis** https://www.youtube.com/watch?v=QozGSS7QY_U

harvested and sold. A lumpy cashflow like this does make it more difficult to put a nest egg away.

Growing businesses

A growing business that is in startup mode or in a rapid-growth phase will be cash-hungry. This is precisely why so many newly established businesses don't make it to a fifth birthday.

Future plans

If your future plans involve significant capital purchases (new vehicles, additional staff, an office in another state etc.), your cash reserves will need to be greater.

Unpaid invoices

How good are your clients at paying on time? If they are like the majority of Australian businesses, the answer will be "not good". Australia holds the world record for late payment of business invoices. Big companies are the worst, so if you are selling to these, your cash reserve will have to be a bit deeper to account for the length of time you must wait for payment.

Your customers

How reliable are your customer contracts? Could your business survive losing one, two, three … of them? Your cash reserve will have to take account of how dependable your cashflow stream is from them. If you read *Small Company, Big Business*, you will find an entire chapter on the subject of contracts – specifically the tricky clauses to watch out for. Contract termination is one of them.

Many big companies use "take it or leave it" contracts. You accept their terms, or don't do a deal. Some include a termination for convenience clause. That is, they can terminate your contract at any time for any reason, but you can't. I always point out that this is an unfair contract term and ask for it to be deleted. That's a subject for another chapter but if your big customers have included such a clause, your revenue may not be as stable as you think.

This is exactly what happened to us when the mining downturn hit. Contract after contract was cancelled. Unfair contract legislation has come into effect since then, and I'm a bit wiser now.

How much cash do you leave on the table? Or, where can you find the cash to save?

I acknowledge that keeping a cash reserve is a difficult task. But there is one place to look for spare cash that you may be overlooking, even though it is directly under your nose. And I can guarantee that it will be there.

It's the cash you leave on the table, or waste, because your company is not performing its daily tasks in the best possible manner. I'm talking about business systems.

This section is a reprise of Section 4 of *Small Company, Big Business*. The reason that this topic makes a repeat performance is simply because it is so critical to long-term business success.

Good business systems, properly implemented, will release additional cash that you can put away in your nest egg. They will also ensure that you know your business thoroughly, in intimate detail – how everything works, what everyone does, what depends on what. That depth of knowledge will also come in very handy when the business faces a threat.

How to find 20–25 percent more revenue

The best way I have found to explain the impact of robust, documented business systems to small-business owners is to invoke author Jay Arthur[14] and his fix-it factory.

---

14   Six Sigma Simplified: Quantum Improvement Made Easy

"Every company has two factories:

- one that creates and delivers your product or service, and
- a hidden 'Fix–it' factory that cleans up all the mistakes and delays that occur in the main factory."

FIX-IT-FACTORY

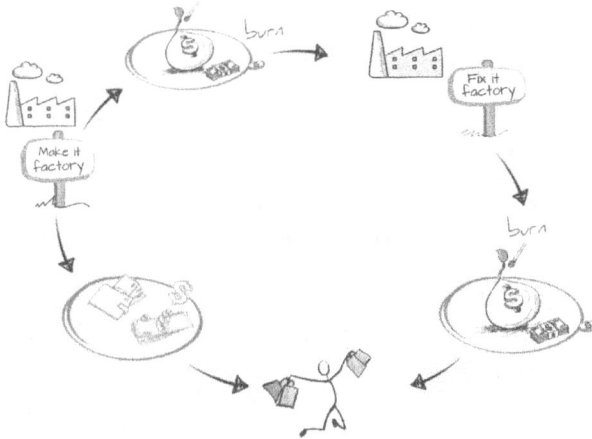

Every time a procedure or process deviates from optimum performance, you waste cash, or leave it on the table. Estimates of how much you can save by implementing and maintaining good business systems are hard to come by. However, from my own experience, and talking to hundreds of other small-business owners, reducing operating costs by as much as 20–25 percent is not unusual.

That huge improvement won't come in one fell swoop – unless you identify some glaring gaps in your business! More likely is a series of smaller improvements will cumulatively add up to a significant leap forward. These are the one-percent improvements.

The case study that follows is based on a USA company. Because they drive on the "wrong" side of the road over there, the opposite applies to us. So, where the case study says, "avoid left turns", that means "avoid right turns" for Australians. Left-hand turns are what we should be doing.

Case Study:
UPS and the campaign against turning left
The giant US-based parcel delivery service UPS instructs its truck drivers to take right-hand turns as opposed to left-hand turns when delivering parcels. (Remember to reverse this for Australia!) The first time I read this, I thought it was a clickbait headline, designed to get me to read an article that would not enlighten me at all on left-hand and right-hand turns while driving a truck.

I was very, very wrong. UPS delivers approximately 18 million packages every single day, so they certainly know something about parcel delivery. UPS has been figuring out how to optimise delivery routes, and minimise time and costs, for a very long time.

UPS started its "anti-left turn" campaign way back in the 1970s when they started to strategically plan their delivery routes rather than allowing truck drivers to figure them out for themselves. In 2008, UPS introduced Orion, a software platform that calculates the best possible delivery route for every truck and every parcel. That's 30,000 route optimisations per minute.

Each route optimisation includes making right-hand turns in preference to left-hand turns unless it can't be avoided. Using Orion and deliberately avoiding left-hand turns has saved UPS millions of dollars, and the planet billions of tonnes of carbon emissions. The data below from CNN says it all.

This one, simple policy has saved:
- *Six to eight miles driven per route*
- *100,000 metric tons of CO_2 every year (equivalent to 21,000 cars taken off the road)*

- *10 million gallons of fuel every year. Just the fuel saving alone is worth $300 to $400 million every year.*

Why Discriminate Against Left-Hand Turns?
Even the Mythbusters were sceptical about the UPS claims on left turns, so they challenged the claim in their iconic tv program. Unlike many other episodes, nothing was blown up in this one, but they did prove that UPS was correct. Right turns are more efficient.

There are two reasons why UPS (and now other delivery companies) favour right-hand turns:

- ***Time*** *– Left turns usually go against the traffic flow, so there is idle time while drivers wait to turn, and more fuel is burned.*
- ***Safety*** *– Turning left results in more car crashes than right turns, and more pedestrians are killed by left-turning vehicles than those turning right.*

Find the "one-percenters"

As a small business owner, you can't expect to save $300 million like UPS does. However, you should be able to save considerable amounts of time and money, and see other noticeable business results, after optimising the so-called "one-percenters".

What I mean by the one-percenters is finding and fixing the small things that could improve the quality of your products and services, reduce the environmental impact of your operation, improve collaboration within your team, and ultimately improve your bottom line.

These one-percenters can lurk in the most unusual places in your business – as the UPS example shows. Be prepared to progress through trial and error. You will need to take measurements pre and post change before you can decide if a specific change is worthwhile.

You will also need to employ creative thinking to find where the opportunities for improvements are hiding. In my own company, we introduced a LEAN Award (LEAN is a systematic method, originally used in manufacturing, to eliminate waste within a system). When someone comes up with a good idea for improvement, they present it to the team, and the winner gets a bottle of wine as a prize. Over time, we've received some brilliant suggestions. Some of these, in fact, had been staring us in the face – if only we'd been looking earlier.

Once you have tracked down your one-percenters, measured their impact and decided to implement the change in your business, the next vital step is to document the change and make sure that everyone knows about it. This is the purpose of your documented business systems: to embed the improved practices in the everyday operations of your business.

Your challenge is to search for the one-percent improvements in your business.

General Electric, the US-based industrial giant, started an event in 2015 called "Unleashing the Power of One Percent". If you don't believe that such small changes really can have such a large, cumulative effect, note what GE's executive announced at the event:

> By unlocking the power of one percent, businesses will be able to enjoy greater savings and efficiency, by just making small changes to the way they do things.

> For instance, a one-percent reduction in fuel will see US$30 billion in saving for aviation companies and a US$66 billion saving in energy costs for power producers.

Finding one percent improvements isn't just for big companies like UPS and GE. Over more than 20 years, our environmental consultancy has experimented with the equipment we use to take groundwater samples.

The objective is that the equipment will be:

- robust, with no breakdowns
- easy to use
- accurate
- environmentally friendly.

The entire configuration of the groundwater-sampling equipment now meets those criteria admirably. It is placed in a canopy on a four-wheel-drive vehicle, with all the associated supplies and equipment placed exactly where it needs to be for easy access. No more walking around and around the 4WD to lift out what is needed. It's all in exactly the right place, every time. These changes have reduced the time and cost required to retrieve a sample.

QUESTION 3: Do you have a single client portfolio?

A single client portfolio is a situation in which you "have all your eggs in one basket" and this is a real time bomb for a resilient business. The bottom line is that if you have just one client, and your one client disappears, so does your business. As a startup, having just one client may be a godsend, but do aim to add more as you grow.

The best way to explain this is with a story, and unfortunately, it's not a happy story.

Case Study:
The rise and fall of Alex's cleaning empire
I found this story in the Sydney Morning Herald some time ago. It's about a small business owner (Alex) who had lost his entire business as well as his house, his car, his fishing gear, everything.

The businessman concerned was a 29-year-old who owned a cleaning company. You have to admire someone who, at that age, has built a company from the ground up and ended up with eight significant cleaning contracts. The only problem was that they were all with the same organisation. Alex had cleaning contracts with eight separate locations of the same fast-food franchise.

One day, he received an email from his client's head office informing him that all contracts were to be terminated. Immediately. Well, it was about 12 hours' notice, but that counts as immediately to me.

The company wished to "thank him for his commitment and service over the past few years", but I'm sure that those kind wishes didn't make Alex feel much better at the time.

Alex bravely started legal proceedings, believing that he had a 24-month contract with the company. The legal battle didn't last long. The giant fast-food franchise company hired a global law firm, and Alex had, well, not much. He quickly ran out of money and his five-year-old company went into liquidation.

This story is a rolled-gold, case-study example of how a small business owner can be plunged from apparent success to bankruptcy in a microsecond when a large customer changes its mind. For the record, Alex had been performing some cleaning and maintenance work for his client when he was asked to expand his services, a very common pathway to the establishment of a small business. Clearly his client was happy with his work because he quickly acquired the aforementioned eight contracts.

The mistake that Alex made was building his business around just one large customer. I know that every small business has to start with just one large buyer (just as we did back in 1997) but staying with just that one client is fraught with danger – as Alex found out.

> *The mistake Alex made was building his business around just one, large customer.*

Your Customer Concentration Ratio

The tale of Alex is, unfortunately, all too common. This enterprising young businessman had allowed his Customer Concentration Ratio (CCR) to remain at 100 percent. Your CCR measures how dependant you are on your biggest customers.

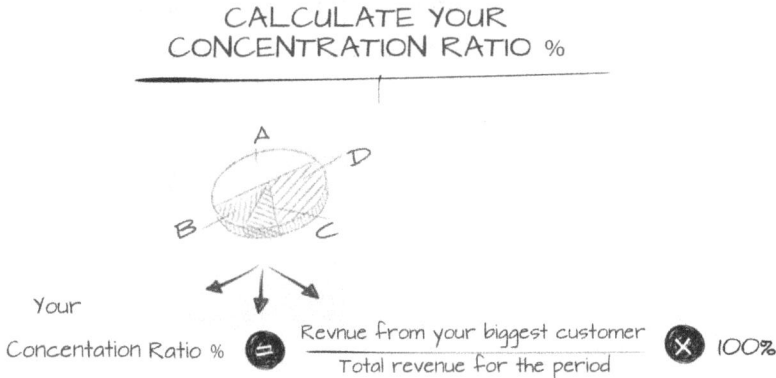

CALCULATE YOUR
CONCENTRATION RATIO %

Your Concentration Ratio % $=$ $\dfrac{\text{Revnue from your biggest customer}}{\text{Total revenue for the period}}$ $\times$ 100%

What's the correct Customer Concentration Ratio?

This is another one of those "how long is a piece of string?" questions. There's no "correct" answer. I do know though, that unless there are extremely unusual circumstances, 100 percent is not the right answer.

The correct number for you will vary with the stage of your business (startup vs mature), what industry you are in, the size of your business, and several other variables. However, if your number is above 80 percent, it's probably worth your while taking time to assess your risk.

You may very well have your family assets encumbered through your business – most small business owners do. (Most banks will only make small-business loans with hard assets as collateral. For most, that means the family home.) Having a high Customer Concentration Ratio is putting all those assets on the line.

Plan on not being Alex.

QUESTION 4: Is your PESTLE up to date?

In *Small Company, Big Business*, I spent an entire chapter on being hyper-aware of your business environment and how to do a PESTLE analysis. With all those letters, it may sound complicated, but it's not. However, it is a critical tool in your resilience toolbox.

A PESTLE analysis is simply a considered look at the things outside your business that can affect it – your external environment.

The letters stand for:

P – Political

E – Economic

S – Social

T – Technological

L – Legal

E – Environmental

Political	Government policies & legislation. Change of Government. War & conflict. Trade agreements.
Economic	Commodity prices. Economic growth/decline. Exchange rates.
Social	Demographic changes/trends. Lifestyle changes. Ethical/religious issues. Consumer preferences.
Technology	Disruptive technologies. Digital technologies. Communication technologies. Innovation potential. Intellectual property.
Legal	Employment law. Health & safety law. Discrimination law. Company law. Taxation Law.
Environmental	Global climate collapse. Natural disasters. Your impact on the environment. Community expectations.

Of course, as we all know now, the environment outside our company can change very rapidly, with dire consequences. So your job as a leader is to tap into every source you can (remember the connectedness I talked about in Chapter 2?), including your team, and try to figure out what those influences are, and how they could affect you.

If you think for a few minutes, COVID-19 featured in every one of those cells above.

POLITICAL   Spats between China and other countries over the origin of the coronavirus sparked trade wars. The different attitudes of world governments led to different health outcomes.

ECONOMIC	There's not much comment needed here. Australia experienced its first recession in 30 years. GDP in some countries dropped by 25 percent or more.
SOCIAL	Lockdowns created huge social shifts. Working from home, home schooling, families seeking a "tree-change", increased family violence, no overseas travel ... The list is virtually endless.
TECHNOLOGY	The online platforms and streaming companies enjoyed a massive boom in their market and profitability. Suddenly, video-conferencing technology was bounding forward in sophistication and functionality. The downturn will also spawn a new crop of technological advances.
LEGAL	Another huge list here. Changes to bankruptcy laws, border closures, limits to movement etc.
ENVIRONMENTAL	The fact that coronavirus burst into the human population is connected to environmental changes.

What can you identify in the PESTLE list that may change in your external environment? If you say nothing, I suggest you are not thinking hard enough!

QUESTION 5: Are you properly insured?

This topic is worthy of its own book. Insurance is key to resilience. Insurance is a huge topic, and fiendishly complicated. Anyone who has worked with a large company or government department will know how important insurance is to those organisations. Anyone who has been affected by a natural disaster will also appreciate how insurance policies can go from last place on your priority list to first place in a millisecond.

A well-thought-out insurance policy can be the difference between life and death for an organisation. A timely example from the coronavirus era is the famous Wimbledon tennis tournament (correctly 'The Championship' at The All England Lawn Tennis and Croquet Club). In 2020, the tournament was cancelled for the first time since World War II. The projected loss of revenue was in the vicinity of $500 million. Even for a wealthy, prestigious organisation such as The All England Lawn Tennis and Croquet Club, that's a significant sum of money. However, the club had learned a valuable lesson back in 2002 when another virus, the SARS virus, terrorised the world. The club took out an insurance policy that included cover for the effect of pandemics. Reportedly, the policy paid out around $226 million to offset the revenue loss.

I am not an insurance specialist. In fact, I have taken my own advice from *Small Company, Big Business*, and found a good insurance broker who understands my business thoroughly. Ask your accountant, lawyer and peers if they know of an insurance broker they would be happy to recommend. The best I can offer is to make sure you have the following, at a minimum:

- vehicle insurance
- plant and equipment/building insurance
- public liability insurance
- professional indemnity insurance
- workers compensation insurance.

Then there is your life insurance, total and permanent disability insurance, key employee insurance, travel insurance, directors insurance, cyber insurance, business interruption insurance, employee fraud insurance, goods in transit insurance etc.

In the next section, I will introduce you to force majeure. It's not strictly insurance, but it deserves a mention in this chapter. Having force majeure clauses in your contracts may be the best insurance you have in a crisis event.

Please seek the assistance of a specialist. How many times do you see news stories where a crisis hits and a business owner has been devastated? And then the interviewer says, "Unfortunately, they did not have insurance …"

Now is the time to get all those policies out of the filing cabinet, have them reviewed, and decide if you need more. In the wake of COVID-19, insurance companies will be going through their policies in forensic detail, and the policy you thought you had may have changed.

QUESTION 6: Do you have the appropriate legal agreements in place?

There is a saying: "Nothing says I love you like a contract". In this section, I am addressing your love for your business. Do you love it enough to have the correct legal contracts in place? There are a thousand things that can affect your business in a crisis situation, but two types of contracts are the most likely to give you trouble if they are triggered: force majeure and employment contracts.

Force Majeure

When an unforeseeable disaster strikes, it is inevitable that some contracts for goods and/or services won't be filled. If your business has flooded, burned to the ground, or if the government says that you must shut your business, you have no choice. And that probably means that you won't be able to deliver on some, or all, of the contracts you have signed in good faith.

So what is your legal position?

I'll preface this by saying that I'm not a lawyer. I think I did a first-year unit of contract law way back at Uni, but that would be the extent of my knowledge. But I know enough to know that not delivering on a contract can be a legal minefield.

Lawyers talk about force majeure as being when something unforeseeable happens that prevents someone from fulfilling a contract.

A force-majeure clause in a contract expressly lets the parties to the contract (that's the buyer and the seller) not be in legal trouble if they can't deliver because something happens that's beyond their control.

Force-majeure clauses will have three elements.

- Trigger event: a list of events that will trigger the force-majeure clause.
- Procedure: what would happen if the event occurs? What to do? Who does what? Notice requirements?
- Consequences: any performance obligations.

There is no standard force-majeure clause, and many contracts won't even have one. Most force-majeure clauses are badly drafted, and/or copied and pasted from elsewhere. After all, they are not relied upon too often. The clause may list some force-majeure events such as a war breaking out or a virus pandemic. It may allow for the contract to be suspended, or even cancelled, or for some parts of the contract to be suspended while other obligations continue.

But before pressing the button to invoke a force-majeure clause, examine the clause carefully for possible consequences. What happens if you do it? The cure just may be worse than the disease. For example, a clause may allow your biggest client to seek out a competitor firm to use if you can't deliver. That would not be an ideal outcome, particularly if you have an exclusive arrangement with the customer. Think about the long-term consequences on your relationships. Is there a way to agree on an outcome that is acceptable to all parties?

What happens if you don't have a force-majeure clause in your contracts? In that case, you dive off into a whole other direction – frustration of a contract. We won't be going down that particular rabbit hole in this book.

I'm not trying to frighten you. I'm just drawing your attention to the important things you need to take care of. This is stuff that you need your lawyer to look at. As I said, I'm no lawyer, but I do know that contract law can be a right beast, especially if a big company's lawyers get involved. If you think there is any chance of force majeure being used, do the following two things.

1. Keep all the relevant documents, take photos and document everything you can.
2. Consult your lawyer.

Employment contracts

I am not going to delve into the intricacies of employment contracts. That's way above my pay grade, and the reason why our company engages a specialist HR organisation to assist us. The bottom line is that every person employed in Australia is covered by minimum working conditions (National Employment Standards), and the complexity escalates from there.

Over the past couple of years, many prominent Australian companies have faced penalties for not paying their employees correctly. I'm cutting them some slack here and sympathising with them. Some employment awards (the document that dictates the employment conditions for a particular group of employees) are so complex that a double PhD in quantum physics would be necessary to understand them. Hence, there is a push by Australian small business lobby groups for a specific small-business award.

When a crisis hits, you will undoubtedly be faced with the prospect of cutting hours, changing work status, standing some people down, or making some employees redundant. Your options will be governed by what is in your employment contracts. The risk planning you undertake will give you some clues as to your possible actions and therefore what you need to cover in the contracts.

I'm willing to wager that you didn't have a global pandemic in mind when your current contracts were drafted. The government agency that oversees work standards in Australia, the Fair Work Commission, has tackled the issue of changing needs in a post-COVID-19 world. Your employee contracts will most likely have to be updated.

Seek out a professional to help you.

QUESTION 7: Do you have a strategy to exit your business and move on?

In the excitement of setting up your own business, it's hard to even think about the possibility of exiting. That's a long way in the future, and in the meantime, there is so much to do just getting through each day.

But all of us will exit one way or another – even if it is in a wooden box. (I've heard many older business owners swear blind that the only way they'll ever leave their business is when they do exactly that!)

We humans are weird creatures. Unlike us, animals prepare for the future. Squirrels are the obvious poster child for the animal kingdom in this regard. They collect nuts all summer so they are ready for winter. They plan ahead.

We, on the other hand, will often wait until a big change is thrust upon us before we start to plan or make a big decision.

Exiting your business is probably one of the bigger decisions you will make during your life, so it makes eminent sense to have a strategy prepared. If the business is profitable, economic conditions are good and you are prepared, you can pull the trigger on your plan and extract maximum value. Conversely, if things go off the rails, you will be able to make a sensible decision that preserves business value and limits losses.

It's not just booms and busts, or pandemics that can upset the best-laid business plans. Disputes between business partners or family members, including divorce, are depressingly common as an exit trigger. Many unnecessary, messy business exits (or collapses) are the end result of business owners having no plans prepared for when things don't go according to the script.

Health issues also feature prominently as an exit trigger. I recounted a story earlier in this book about my experience of being carried off an aeroplane and whisked off to hospital. That certainly focussed my mind on reviewing our own exit plans.

Burnout comes under the health issues category as well – especially for older business owners. Many of us tend to forget that we are not 30 anymore and can't go at quite the same pace as we used to. Burnout is also a symptom of a business not operating correctly – one of those businesses that has a fix-it factory, and it's over capacity.

Author Stephen Covey's advice to "Begin with the end in mind" is appropriate here.[15] The time to start planning your exit from your business is the day you start it.

If things go off the rails, you will be able to make
a sensible decision that preserves business value
and limits losses.

---

15   Stephen Covey, *The 7 Habits of Highly Effective People*

Hopefully, if you have gone through the 7 questions above, you will be in a better position to weather the storm of a crisis – whatever shape it may take.

Chapter 4

10 Steps to Deal With a Crisis – Without Freezing Like a Rabbit in the Headlights

Chapter 2 described the attributes of a resilient business. These are the skills and tools you need to equip yourself with to prepare for battle – your business armour.

Preparation is terrific, but what do you do when the boom turns to bust or a crisis actually hits? When the clients you thought were solid, suddenly disappear into thin air? When your bank balance starts to dwindle?

This is the point at which we can potentially turn into a rabbit staring straight into the headlights of a huge, economic bus bearing down upon us at great speed.

From my own, sometimes unfortunate, experience and my conversations with hundreds (thousands?) of business owners, the material in this section is my take on what we need to do once the crisis hits.

Our aim through this period is to stay solvent, stay sane and prepare for the post-despair phase of the bust. The upturn will come …

Step 1: Start with your Circle of Control.

As I explained in the introduction, our brains trigger the fight, flight or freeze response in a crisis, and we can become incapable of making any decisions – let alone sensible ones.

I'm sure that many of you reading this book will have heard of Steven Covey's book *The 7 Habits of Highly Effective People*.

If you have, you will know about the Circle of Concern and the Circle of Influence.

A Circle of Concern is all the things that we have to worry about in our lives. The kids, our health, what's happening at work, house prices, global warming, bombings, pandemics, the plight of refugees etc.

Some of those issues we can do something about, and some we can't. So, inside the Circle of Concern is the Circle of Influence. In here reside those concerns that we can do something about to influence an outcome.

Jane Taylor[16] has added a **Circle of Control** to Steven Covey's diagram. The diagram now looks like this:

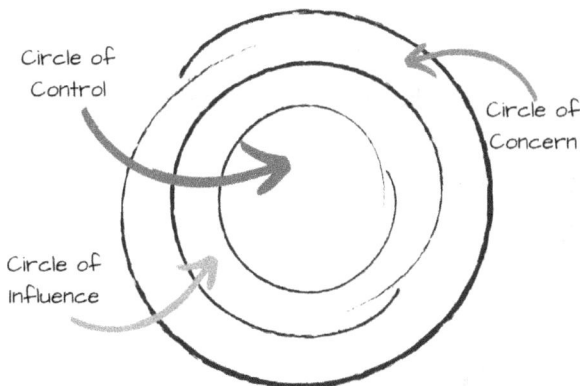

Circle of Control

Circle of Concern

Circle of Influence

16   https://www.habitsforwellbeing.com/the-circle-of-concern-and-influence/

In the middle, the Circle of Control, are the things that you can directly control, and that you make a positive decision to do so. This is where you need to concentrate your efforts and emotional energy.

If I use the example of my concern about climate change, I can control my consumption patterns. I can buy produce in bulk to reduce the amount of plastic I buy, live in a house that doesn't require huge air-conditioners to make it habitable, drive a fuel-efficient vehicle and so on.

Stay in the Circle of Control

When our business is sideswiped by a busted boom, a natural disaster, or some other crisis, we suddenly have a whole new menu of issues added to our Circle of Concern. There is a cornucopia of threats for us to fight, flee from or freeze in the face of, just as described in the introduction.

Lots of things in the Circle of Concern.

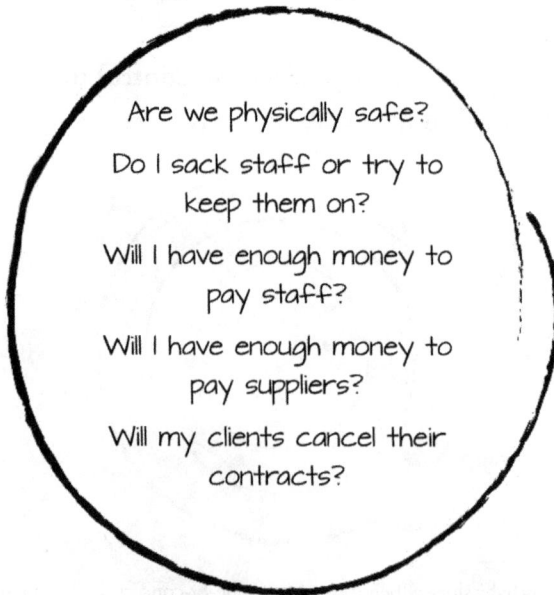

Are we physically safe?

Do I sack staff or try to keep them on?

Will I have enough money to pay staff?

Will I have enough money to pay suppliers?

Will my clients cancel their contracts?

To survive whatever it is that is threatening your business, you must concentrate on the Circle of Control. That is where you need to spend your time and emotional energy.

What happened when the talk of lockdowns started in response to the coronavirus pandemic? We saw clearly how many people spent their money, time and emotional energy. People raided supermarket shelves, vented their frustrations online with 'unsocial' social-media posts, listened to and perpetuated untruths etc.

Your small business has enormous opportunity to be an influencer, and you certainly do have things that you control.

Step 2: Cut early and cut hard – look after the cash.

This is the most important item within your Circle of Control. Attend to this first, because this is the main issue that elicits real 'rabbit in the headlight' behaviour, where you avoid looking at the bank account, don't return calls, and sit frozen until you lose the opportunity to take control at all.

When a crisis hits, the usual sequence of events is that revenue declines (or precipitously declines, or even disappears altogether), but costs remain sticky. All those overhead costs are still there – wages, insurance policies, rent, lease payments etc. – but all of a sudden there is no offsetting revenue.

Examine your expenses and cut early and cut hard. At this early stage, your first priority is protecting your working capital – effectively, your cash. Variable costs will usually be more visible and easier to reduce. Cast a critical eye over all costs. Do you really need to make that trip, or travel to that conference? Do you really need to hire any extra people now that the downturn has arrived? Can that training course wait?

And don't stop at the big items. (Remember those one-percent changes?)

I know this seems trivial, but are there any subscriptions to magazines or software platforms that you are paying for but you don't really need any more? Many of us have found some of these lurking on the credit card bill. In particular, look for the ones where you signed up for a 14-day free trial but forgot to cancel before the free-trial period was over. (I plead guilty.)

As another example, how long is it since you reviewed all your telephone bills? Are you still paying for a mobile plan that George, who left two years ago, had for his work phone? That's not as silly as it sounds. Many years ago, I was working for a company in Brisbane when we moved to a new building. When the phones were being moved, the accountants found that the company had been paying line rental for over 10 years for a line that wasn't used.

In short, go through your profit and loss account, line by line, and hunt down the little leaks that, together, can add up to a huge cashflow out of the business. Work with your accountant. They know your business and will have lots of strategies you can implement to preserve that precious working capital.

Of course, the really hard one in this category is your team. Do you need to terminate some employees? Perhaps some can take leave without pay? If so, who? Maybe you can consider reduced working hours?

For a small-business owner, whose employees often become more like family members than staff, this is terrible and it really, really hurts. But the alternative may be worse. At best, you may find yourself working very hard and losing money yourself, just to keep others in work.

Don't be a rabbit and freeze. Act fast and keep your business.

I have written in the past about how our legal system operates to virtually ensure that if a small business has cashflow issues, insolvency follows. Once the process starts with a bank or creditor taking action, there is virtually no chance for a small business to restructure and recover.

During the COVID-19 pandemic, there were some changes to insolvency and corporations laws, but please don't ask me to explain them. That's what your accountant and your lawyer are for.

What I can do though is plead with you that if a crisis gets you into a bad place, speak up, seek help and take control. Once a small business gets into a cashflow crisis, the 'system' often takes over, and any hope of recovery is lost. The end is inevitable and usually results in the owner losing control of the business, as well as personal assets. A large part of this process is understanding yourself and how you react under stress. If you recognise those signals, you will be much better equipped to seek appropriate assistance before the stress of the situation becomes overwhelming and action becomes virtually impossible.

Step 3: In a crisis, your client's needs and habits will change. You have to change too.

Your customer's needs

If you have ever encountered any leadership or management training, you will most likely have been introduced to Maslow's hierarchy of needs. It's a psychological theory devised in 1943 by Abraham Maslow.

His framework has become a staple of not only academic research and studies of society, but all leadership and management training as well.

At its core, this framework outlines five motivational needs of humans, depicted as a hierarchical pyramid. As humans reach each level of this hierarchy, they become satisfied and move upward to the next level.

In order from the bottom to the top, these levels are as follows.

1. Physiological needs. These are our basic needs: food, water, clothing and shelter.
2. Safety and security. These are our health, employment, property, family and social stability.
3. Love and belonging. Friendship, intimacy and a sense of connection.
4. Self-esteem. These include confidence, achievement and the respect of others.
5. Self-actualisation. This is where we strive to realise or fulfil our full potential and talents.

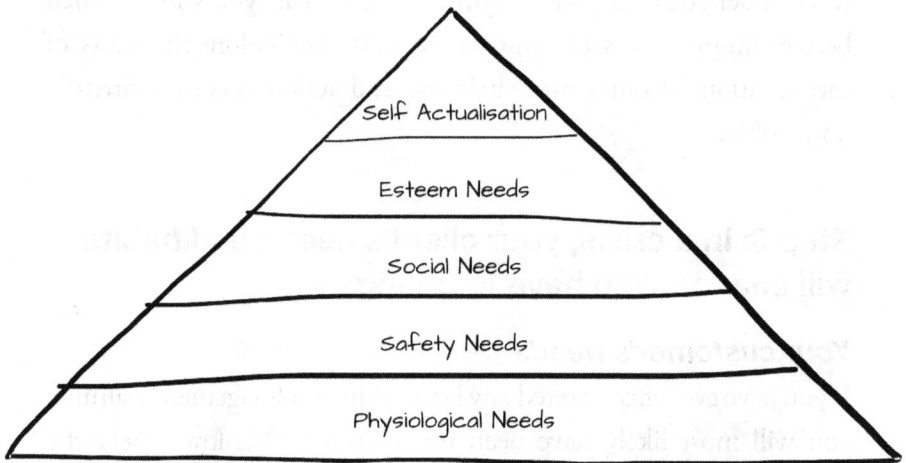

Self Actualisation

Esteem Needs

Social Needs

Safety Needs

Physiological Needs

As business owners, we need to understand which level we serve with our product or service.

Before the COVID-19 pandemic, the majority of Australians were working on achieving the upper-three levels.

Then COVID-19 showed up and our lives were turned upside down. In a matter of days, many of us were knocked back down to the first two levels of the hierarchy. We were facing potential short-ages of food and supplies, threats to our health, separation from loved ones, and loss of income. In bushfires, floods and cyclones, it is our physiological and safety needs that are threatened.

As business owners, we need to be sensitive to where our customers are in a crisis. Are they still coping with their physiological and their safety and security needs after losing their jobs or business? Or are their higher level needs not being met because of the various restrictions? If you are aiming your marketing at the top levels, are you being sensitive to those still searching for the bottom-two levels, while still connecting with your target market?

An excellent example of responding sensitively to a crisis is the music and entertainment industry hosting virtual live-stream performances. Festivals and performances are traditionally a place for people to gather and connect with one another, but these were all abruptly cancelled. The industry quickly organised to move these events online which allowed fans to enjoy performances and connect through live chats, serving the upper levels of the hierarchy. At the same time, audiences were acutely aware of the restrictions and danger preventing them from live participation.

Your customer's habits

Psychologists tell us that it takes an average of 66 days to change a habit.[17] If that is correct, a large proportion of the world's popula-tion had ample time to change their habits starting in 2020.

According to the global consulting firm McKinsey, an astonishing 75 percent of US consumers altered their shopping habits as a result of the pandemic and lockdowns.[18]

---

17   https://www.sciencealert.com/how-long-it-takes-to-break-a-habit-according-to-science
18   https://www.mckinsey.com/business-functions/marketing-and-sales/our-insights/
     the-great-consumer-shift-ten-charts-that-show-how-us-shopping-behavior-is-
     changing?cid=other-eml-onp-mip-mck&hlkid=9efb74533cc8462d9a7b4fc47
     3b206a1&hctky=&hdpid=5114673d-1bbe-4287-90df-99cef35a3577

Amongst others, the following changes were revealed by the research.

- Online shopping boomed.
- Brand loyalty faded. Thirty-six percent of consumers tried a new brand, and 73 percent of these intended to continue using the new brands.
- Hygiene became a major factor influencing shopping habits.
- Customers sought value for money.
- Customers spent money on their homes.

The lesson we need to take on board as small-business owners is that a crisis will bring about changes in what your customers are doing, what they are looking for, and how they are feeling.

The successful business is the one that is sensitive to those changes and reacts accordingly.

Step 4: Protect your reputation. Your customers are watching you. Don't be a jerk.

In a crisis, it is important to ensure your business reputation remains intact.

One of the topics that I write and speak about regularly is business ethics, particularly the ethics surrounding the big business–small business relationship. The power difference between these two parties is considerable and results in unethical behaviour by the more powerful party in far too many instances. We only need to cast our minds back to the Australian Royal Commission into Misconduct in the Banking, Superannuation and Financial Services Industry (the Banking Royal Commission) of 2018–2019 to see cringeworthy examples of corporate bad behaviour.

Unfortunately, that bad behaviour is not limited to large

organisations (but being large, they can do a lot more damage). In a crisis, there are opportunities for all sorts of businesses to benefit themselves at the expense of others.

But it's a bad idea. The way you behave during a crisis will be remembered for a very, very long time by your customers, your peers and your stakeholders.

The way you behave during a crisis will be remembered for a very, very long time by your customers, your peers, and your stakeholders.

I clearly remember the coffee vendor that put up the price of a coffee to $11 per cup during the floods we experienced in 2010–2011. Yes, I know all about supply and demand, but more than doubling the cost of a coffee, especially when cash was simply not obtainable, didn't go down well. (The simple pleasure of a good coffee can do wonders in a physical crisis situation.) Many locals have never purchased a coffee there again.

The COVID-19 pandemic was replete with examples, starting with outright exploitation of fear and falsehoods. For example, former chef Pete Evans advertised a light machine that would help fight the virus. Fortunately, the relevant authorities caught up with him and issued a large (but not large enough?) fine.

Across the world, governments rapidly injected billions of dollars in cash into economies to keep them functioning. Unfortunately, some company owners and managers saw these funds as an addition to cashflow that was available for dividend increases and executive bonuses. Several Australian companies saw the gap and did exactly that, and stimulus funds finished up in the hands of shareholders and directors.

Other companies took the opportunity to lengthen their payment terms, including to small businesses. Others, in particular clothes retailers, made it onto the "naughty" list when they cancelled orders wholesale from their garment suppliers in Asia. While the first reaction in a downturn is to cancel, cancel, cancel, that has serious repercussions down their supply chain. Their product is often manufactured in low-wage factories in countries such as Bangladesh. Losing orders means thousands of women out of work in those countries. Oxfam Australia called on these companies to think a little further, and at least pay the wage component of their orders to prevent sudden poverty amongst garment workers. According to Oxfam, the wages component of a $10 T-shirt is just 4 cents – not beyond the capacity of large organisations.[19]

Kmart Australia asked for a 30 percent discount on orders that had already been manufactured. (The request was later withdrawn – presumably after negative press coverage.)

Other brands, however, took the longer view and committed to honour all orders that had already been produced, or were already in production. (Adidas, H&M, Marks & Spencer, Nike and Uniqlo were on the "nice" list.)

You may remember the story about the non-prescription painkiller medication Nurofen and how they were caught using misleading advertising for their painkillers. That story is a good reminder for every business owner that business reputation is a fragile thing that takes a long time to build but is easily broken.

In a nutshell, the tablets that Nurofen advertised as being for specific types of pain were, in fact, just the same old Nurofen in every packet. The packets proclaimed that the active ingredient could go "straight to the site of the pain". I guess, in a way, it does – but it also goes straight to every other part of your body as well.

---

19 https://www.abc.net.au/news/2020-05-13/australian-retailers-delay-supplier-payments-amid-coronavirus/12236458

Anyone with a high-school level of chemistry (or probably less) and a few moments to read the back of the packets could tell you this, but it took Australia's legal system from 2011 to 2017 to get the offending advertising under control. The Federal Court ordered the company to remove all the misleading packaging within three months. The makers of Nurofen were told to withdraw the product way back in 2011, but they chose to ignore the order and just keep on going until 2017.

Why would a large, trusted brand name continue to sell a product that it had been told to remove from sale by a government authority?

There are thousands of other examples of a trusted brand choosing to put its corporate reputation at risk. Another infamous example of corporate hubris was Volkswagen cheating on emissions tests for their vehicles.[20]

Those of us with businesses further down the supply chain cannot be so bold. We must do everything we can to protect our brand. One thing that our potential (and actual) big customers will not accept in their supply chain is risk and that includes reputation risk. If you screw up, you can be sure that your big customers will cut you loose very quickly so their potential damage is isolated.

If you screw up, your big customers will cut you loose very quickly.

So, for most of us, the possibility of reputation risk has real financial consequences such as losing real contracts and being

---

20   https://www.bbc.com/news/business-34324772

barred from ever dealing with that company, or even an entire industry, again.

I spoke recently with a procurement manager from a large company who had awarded a smaller supplier a substantial project. The smaller supplier took the up-front payment, but then failed to deliver for a whole 12 months. Of course, that put the big company off-side with its customers. I doubt that supplier will ever get another chance in that industry.

A short-term gain may be attractive and very tempting, but the long-term pain of a damaged reputation will be worse.

Step 5: Your survival depends on your external team, so use them.

In *Small Company, Big Business*, I talk about your external business team. These are the professionals you engage to help your business succeed: your accountant, lawyer, financier, insurance broker etc. These are the people you need to be listening to for advice – not random Facebook accounts (see following section).

For every crisis, there will be a government reaction: a grant, concessional loan, business support payment etc. Your task is to contact your external team, seek their counsel, and then implement their advice. For example, getting the wrong advice on how to access and use the various government incentives that poured into the COVID-affected economy could have cost your business dearly, both in dollars and in potential legal consequences.

The other players you need to survive are your internal team.

Step 6: Trust with your employees is critical for surviving a crisis.

There is an annual research report that comes out every January/ February called the Edelman Trust Barometer.[21] I look forward to it every year because it provides such interesting insights into what is happening in the world.

To trust someone, or an institution, we want them to be both competent and ethical. In fact, we place three times as much importance on ethics as we do on competence according to the Edelman survey.

The 2020 survey showed that people world-wide don't think ANY institution is both competent and ethical.

- Both government and the media were seen as both incompetent and unethical.
- NGOs were seen as ethical but not competent.
- Business was seen as competent but not ethical.

Globally, we are not trusting what we're being told by government and the media. This lack of trust is showing up in share-market drops and appalling behaviour in shops, where shoppers literally came to blows over toilet paper in supermarket aisles.

So the trust that has been squandered by government, the media and yes, business, over the past decade is coming home to roost.

So what does this mean for us as business owners?

Here's the kicker. Family business is the most trusted business sector. Business owners, and it seems particularly family business owners, are our employee's best bet for reliable information.

---

21   Global communications firm Edelman conducts an annual world-wide survey on how much people trust the various institutions in their lives – Government, media, business and not-for-profits. The survey has run for over 20 years, and is a highly-respected source of information.

I'm certainly not suggesting that we all become experts and give our employees advice. But measured, calm and forward-looking responses will do a whole lot better for everyone than public displays of panic.

While our teams are looking to us for reliable information during a crisis, we in turn can recruit their efforts to get out of the trenches. Many hands make light work, and many heads make for lots of ideas.

Just above, I talk about how your customers and other stakeholders are watching your reactions to a crisis situation, so it's a good idea to not be a jerk. Your team is one of those stakeholders. They are frightened, just as your customers and suppliers are. They are watching your behaviours, and they need clear and trustworthy communication from you. Incidentally, this is based on psychological research, not just me making it up. Being transparent, empathetic and honest is the mark of good leadership. That doesn't mean that you can't deliver bad news – you may have to. But bad news delivered from a trusted source will land much easier.

In summary, just be kind.

Step 7: Dust off your strategic plan.

I'm tempted to say, find that 2020 strategic plan that you were advised to prepare, including by me, and put it in the recycle bin. (I'll bet that you are tempted to do this too!)

To some extent that's true. We didn't foresee a global pandemic – well, at least I didn't! But that's exactly why I would never advise anyone to prepare one of those old-fashioned, hundreds of pages long, business plans. The sort I was taught to do when I did my MBA back in the 1990s.

A business plan should be flexible enough to change as circumstances change. Yes, the implementation details will be different now, maybe the entire plan is different now, but I suspect not if you are using tools like the Business Model Canvas. [22]

In Chapter 3, I wrote about keeping your PESTLE analysis up to date. In the throes of a crisis, you may be scratching to get time to get a decent meal or cup of coffee, but it actually is important to keep what's happening in your external environment top of mind – not just for the dangers but for the opportunities it may present. There are innumerable examples of companies doing a pivot during the COVID-19 pandemic (to the point where we were all thoroughly sick of hearing the word "pivot").

- Gin distilleries took diversification to the extreme by starting to manufacture hand sanitiser.
- Fashion brands took a left turn into medical scrubs and face masks.
- Two South Australian companies that had previously worked together to produce luxury speakers collaborated to manufacture face shields. The "Ned's-head" face shields were named in honour of Australian bushranger Ned Kelly. (You have to admire the Australian sense of humour in invoking the name of a famous criminal to help in a pandemic crisis.)[23]

Business plans are not etched in stone for a reason.

Step 8: Don't let the line go dead.

Keep in touch with your customers. If you follow any of my writing, you will know that my central theme is helping small business

---

22 The Business Model Canvas is a strategic planning tool that shows your entire business model on a page https://www.strategyzer.com/canvas/business-model-canvas to help you, the underlying business plan will still be your guide.

23 https://www.smartcompany.com.au/coronavirus/these-two-south-australian-companies-have-pivoted-from-luxury-speakers-to-face-shields-to-meet-coronavirus-shortages/

and big business to work together. You need each other but speak different languages.

You will also know that if you're a small business, landing a big client isn't an easy thing to do. So, for those of you who have made the breakthrough and now have one of those big names as a client, this is a critical time for you.

Earlier, I talked about how big companies hate risk in their supply chains. In fact, that's one of the big reasons why they won't engage you as a supplier in the first place. An economic disruption or other crisis that disrupts supply chains doesn't change that. In fact, it will heighten their risk detectors to maximum setting. (More about risk in supply chains in Chapter 6.)

Your task is to keep in touch with your contacts at your big-company client – in fact ALL your clients. Let them know whether you can or cannot meet your obligations. If there will be delays, let them know. If you're still able to supply as normal, they will probably give you a big hug.

Your big-company contact is probably scared. Scared whether they will still have a job, or that they and their family are safe, just like everyone is scared when a crisis hits. Keep in touch and keep the communications going. Don't let the line go dead, or it may never come alive again.

STEP 9: Check on what has happened to your competitors.

Any crisis, no matter how widespread, will not affect all businesses the same. During the 2008 GFC, businesses supplying to the resources industry barely felt a bump in the economic road. Their turn came later, in 2012–2013, when the rest of Australia was starting to pick themselves up off the floor and the resources industry fell into a big, black hole.

Check around your industry and assess what the effect has been on your competition. Are they coping, or not? How are they reacting? Are they cutting prices, changing markets, or supplying to other areas or a smaller geographic area? There are a million different possibilities and each one will be changing your competitive landscape.

During the resources collapse, our small environmental firm suddenly found that some of the giant, multinational consultancy firms were venturing into our patch and bidding on projects that would have been considered too small to bother with mere months previously. In addition, they were quoting extraordinarily cheap rates, financed by a loss-leader strategy and putting graduates who had been out of Uni for five minutes onto projects way above their pay grade. Needless to say, that created some real difficulties for us, even though we knew that the quality of work was being compromised.

On the other hand, the 2020 COVID-19 pandemic worked in the exact opposite direction. All our interstate-based competitors could no longer travel to Queensland. Even the city-based Queensland competition was constrained in how much they could travel.

All of a sudden, for some aspects of our work, we had our local patch to ourselves. Of course, we knew that there would be an end to this window of opportunity, but we did our best to capitalise on it while we could!

COVID-19 translated into an unexpected opportunity, especially for regional businesses. Those providing an essential service, and therefore still operating, had an opportunity. Some that had been unable to get on the radar of a potential client because "they already had a supplier in place", would now find the client very receptive. A great example of this was domestic air travel. While it was being restricted by many large companies, smaller charter flights stepped in to fill this void for some resources companies. Smaller charter flights provided a way for those resources companies to protect their employees from high-risk areas such as taxis, airports and public aircraft.

During a crisis, it's as much about mindset as it is about ingenuity, so I would encourage all small businesses to think outside the doom and gloom and explore new relationships and new client opportunities wherever possible.

STEP 10: Be (reliably) informed.

It's always important to be reliably informed, but it's critical during a crisis. To refresh your memory, re-read the section on connectedness from Chapter 2.

When a crisis with wide impact hits (think floods, bushfires, GFC, pandemic etc.), there is usually wall-to-wall, 24-hour coverage of the event, whatever it may be. There will be much pontification on what it all means, the extent of the damage etc. There is absolutely no way you can avoid the chatter on radio, tv and social media, even with your filters on. And that's exactly what most of it is: chatter. A lot of it will be speculation and at worst, there are the straight-out falsehoods that emerge from the murky depths of the internet and infest our lives.

In the area I live, there were not one but two false positive coronavirus cases diagnosed during the 2020 pandemic. The second case, where sadly, the person was deceased, was splashed all over the Australian (and possibly international) media for days. I cannot begin to express my disgust at the ridiculous, vile chatter that erupted, including from people who had absolutely nothing to do with the case, and from people who did not live anywhere near the area. Tearing a community apart is not the way to win in a crisis as the final, inglorious days of the Trump administration in the USA amply demonstrated.

To deal with the crisis at hand, you need a clear head. To achieve this, you need to ignore the chatter and turn to trusted sources. If you find yourself being overwhelmed by the sheer mass of information out there, choose a handful of outlets and check them once or twice a day. Don't have them running in the background causing information overload. At the very least, turn off all notifications on the computer and devices. There's enough bad news around without being bombarded with it constantly. Many outlets offer daily email digests. Unsubscribe from newsletters you are not reading and subscribe to that handful of trusted outlets. Watch the ABC or other credible news sources. Be aware of what's happening in the economy, in markets, in the world but understand that social media is **not** a reliable news source.

Advice from the big end of town: Deloitte's lessons in crisis

Global consultancy firm Deloitte produced a comprehensive report summarising their lessons from the SARS virus outbreak in 2003, the 2008 Global Financial Crisis, and the Japanese earthquake of 2011.

In this report, they outline 15 critical practices in order to alleviate damage to your business during a volatile crisis. I have summarised these below, however, I highly recommend reading the report in full.[24]

1. **Ensure you have a robust framework for managing supply chain risk.**
    Understand the financial risks of your key trading partners, customers and suppliers. Do you know if any of your clients are running into trouble and may not be able to pay their invoices?

---

24   https://www2.deloitte.com/content/dam/Deloitte/global/Documents/About-Deloitte/gx-COVID-19-managing-cash-flow-in-crisis.pdf

2. **Ensure your own financing remains viable.**

Do not assume that your previous financing options will be available to you now. Communicate with your financier to clarify which options will remain open and engage in scenario planning to accurately understand how much cash you may require.

3. **Focus on the cash-to-cash conversion cycle.**

Rather than focussing solely on your P&L, shift your attention to your balance sheet. Examine your payables, receivables and inventory.

4. **Think like a CFO, across the organisation.**

Rather than focussing only on day-to-day operations, take a helicopter view of the business. How can you reduce your working capital requirements?

5. **Revisit your variable costs.**

Are all your variable costs still necessary? Some of them may be variable but not totally necessary in the new environment.

6. **Revisit capital investment plans.**

Can some planned capital expenditures be delayed or scrapped altogether? Do you need to purchase that new vehicle or equipment?

7. **Focus on inventory management.**

In uncertain times, you may find yourself with excess inventory or even shortages. (Harvey Norman sold out of computer screens during COVID-19 as so many people started working from home.) Existing inventory levels and ordering processes may have to be completely reviewed.

8. **Extend payables intelligently.**

    An obvious way of extending your working capital is delaying payments to your suppliers, but this suggestion has only made it into this book because it's on the Deloittes' list. I have spent decades counselling big companies to not do this, so I can hardly recommend it myself. If you do, proceed with extreme caution. Burning bridges with your suppliers in a crisis is not a smart business move.

9. **Manage and expedite receivables.**

    Put your invoicing and accounts receivable processes on steroids. If you have some clients who aren't so good at paying on time, pay particular attention to them. If necessary, cease working for them. At this point, your working capital is gold, so tying it up with a non-paying customer is not going to work for you.

10. **Consider alternate supply chain financing options.**

    Offering a discount for early payment to your customers may be worth considering. Cash in your bank account is better than cash in theirs. There are also commercial organisations that will take over your accounts receivable book and pay you earlier than the client would. They charge a fee, of course, but again, the object is to get cash in.

11. **Audit payables and receivables transactions.**

    This is the line-by-line examination of your profit and loss account that I referred to earlier. Are you taking advantage of early payment discounts? Is there an alternative to the product you are using? Are you billing out everything that you should be? If an item has been purchased for a client project, is it being allocated to that client as a recoverable cost, or simply to admin expenses?

12. Understand your business interruption insurance.

I touched on the topic of insurance in Chapter 3. Now is the time to reap the benefits of being prepared. Your business interruption insurance in particular may well be a critical cashflow lifeline now.

13. Consider alternate or non-traditional revenue streams.

When the mining industry collapsed in 2012, 4T Consultants had to find other market segments to serve and new products to sell. Through going back to our agricultural roots (pardon the pun) and creating some new business partnerships, we were able to get through. The COVID-19 pandemic saw thousands upon thousands of companies following this path. Fine-dining restaurants adopted take-away. Gin distilleries manufactured hand sanitiser, car companies manufactured ventilation units, and the examples go on.

14. Convert fixed to variable costs, where possible.

Maybe you can outsource some tasks within your business rather than having a permanent employee. Could you rent an office instead of owning a building? Your trusted accountant will be able to help with this aspect of cash preservation because they understand your business, and there could be tax implications from any decisions.

15. Think beyond your four walls.

Or in other terms, think outside the box. All the one percent improvements you make will help but don't limit yourself to just your own business. Your suppliers and customers should be part of the conversation as well. As with point 8, simply squeezing your suppliers is a blunt instrument, which may come back to bite you later. Many large companies will have a separate company/division that will step in and actually purchase critical suppliers that are experiencing difficulty. (We saw this happen during the mining downturn.)

Chapter 5
What Happens Now? Coming Out the Other Side

In Chapters 3 and 4, I have written what I know and have experienced about preparing for and living through crises of various types. What to do in the shock or "rabbit in the headlights phase". But eventually, the crisis will abate, and it will be time to start the recovery phase.

Once again, we need to go to our Circle of Control. What can we actually control about our future business? A lot will depend upon our external environment, things such as what governments do etc. But we can control our own assumptions about our businesses.

Revisit the boom and bust graph. What can we expect?

From "Rabbit in the headlights" to recovery

Eventually, you will exit the shock, or "rabbit in the headlights", phase of the crisis where you may have frozen with shock and fear. Next are the "assess the damage" and "recovery" phases where we have emerged from the shock, and need to get on with our businesses.

Crashes follow a set pattern. The first crash I survived was October 1987. It was a crash in the stock market and the economy, and it looked like this.

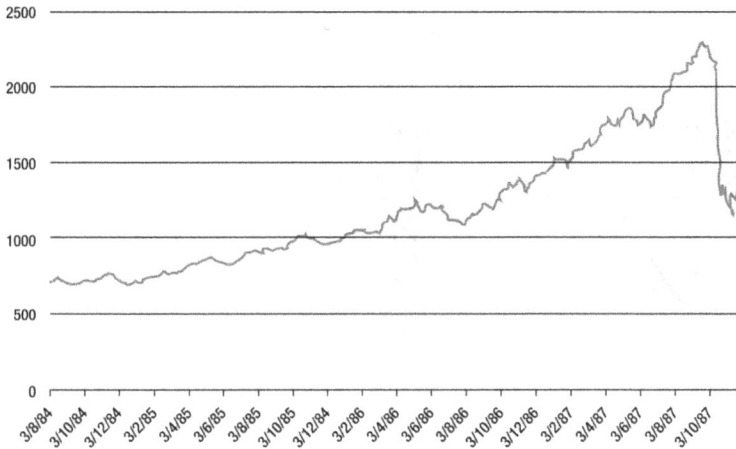

Australian All Ordinaries Index from August 1984 to November 1987

After that horrendous drop in share prices and the bounce you can see at the end of graph, many thought the worst was behind them.

But that wasn't the case.

The following cartoon sums up what really happened, and every recovery unfolds as a time of turbulence.

By necessity, the content in this section is skewed towards our experiences so far from the COVID-19 pandemic. It's no use receiving advice on how to extract yourself from the 1987 stock market crash! Of course, this content will be relevant to the next crisis, and the one after that.

In September 2020, Australia fell into recession for the first time in almost 30 years.

Recessions come in various shape – there's U, W, V and L shaped recessions, varying by how long the recession lasts. Whatever shape the recession finishes up being, there will be opportunities.

While most governments were cautious at first about what the COVID-19 pandemic meant, on the whole, they did react quickly once they saw the magnitude of the threat.

Then, within days and weeks, everything started happening.

The impossible became possible.

- Homeless people were housed in hotels.
- Childcare became accessible (free with some caveats).
- A Universal Basic Income Lite was introduced in the form of JobSeeker and JobKeeper programs.
- Telehealth services became eligible for Medicare Benefits Schedule.
- People worked from home.

One of the greatest changes in the pandemic crisis was the shift to working from home. For some, that brought a lifestyle improvement. No sitting in traffic for hours on the daily commute, casual (sometimes too casual?) dressing, more time with kids, and greater freedom about how their work got done. (The pet vote was firmly for working from home. Having owners available all day for pats and attention was heaven.) For these people, the ability to offer remote work in a business became a powerful recruiting tool.

For others, WFH was close to torture, and they couldn't wait to get back to a bustling office.

We need a new leadership in a new environment

However our own businesses decide to organise work in the future, if work from home is involved, that will require good, and different, leadership. Given that leadership is, on the whole, sadly lacking anyway, we have to wonder how this will pan out. Try this exercise. Open LinkedIn, and type "Leadership training" into the search box. The day I tried it, LinkedIn returned almost 19 million results. Forbes magazine tells us that, in 2019, USD\$366 billion (yes, with a b) was spent on leadership training globally.[25]

The big question is if we have so much leadership education, how come our leaders are generally so bad?

Negotiating the exit from any crisis and/or recession requires strong leadership. Unfortunately, the definition of strong leadership for many is "the same leadership that got us into trouble in the first place". (For example, there is no sign that the leaders who took us into the 2008 Global Financial Crisis have changed their modus operandi at all.)

So, one of our first tasks as business owners is to assess how our

---

25   https://www.forbes.com/sites/chriswestfall/2019/06/20/leadership-development-why-most-programs-dont-work/#5e1d5a2461de

leadership must change and adapt to the new circumstances – whatever they may be. That is where those skills I discussed back in Chapter 2 come in. The adaptive and proactive leaders will innovate, try different things, and be the leaders that the Edelman Trust Barometer employees are looking for.

Examine your assumptions

When a crisis hits, the world changes. Sometimes a little; sometimes a lot. Sometimes it's just our own world, and sometimes it's everybody's. In the wake of the Australian bushfires of early 2020, entire communities were devastated. This level of disruption caused us to question many aspects of our lives.

One element I would invite you to examine is your assumptions about business growth. Grow is what we are told we must do. Remember "Jobs and Growth, Jobs and Growth"?

I contend that growth isn't compulsory. That's not to say that your business doesn't mature, or stays forever in the chaotic state that typifies a lot of startups. It merely means that you take a conscious decision to stay small, or at a certain size. I know plenty of small businesses and solo-preneurs turning over significant amounts of money and doing very well.

So you don't need to feel guilty because you don't aspire to be the next Google or Apple. "Business growth" is a bit of an elephant in the room. It is perfectly acceptable for you to make your own, rational decision on what YOU want your business to look like.

Digital economy

When the COVID-19 lockdown started, our first collective reaction was shock, then wondering how we were all going to communicate. Apart from my own speaking engagements, I have friends who are professional speakers. They saw their next two years' worth of bookings vanish into thin air.

Then we remembered video conferencing – Skype, Zoom, GoToMeeting etc. Our next step was to learn how to use the technology, and judging by most of the meetings I attended, that was a bit of an uphill battle for some. How many of you spent the first 15 minutes of a video session saying, "Can you hear me?", or "I can see you but I can't hear you". One Facebook meme I saw compared the average video conference to a séance.

The point is that digitisation came screaming into our lives even more than it already had. In the words of the Australian Small Business and Family Enterprise Ombudsman, Kate Carnell, "Digitisation is now essential for a small business to be truly competitive". I would go further and say that digitisation is essential for a small busines to survive.

Research firm PwC[26] has been studying and following digitisation trends for decades. Their conclusions never change: digitisation is imperative and adds billions of dollars of value to economies. Given the supply chain shocks of the COVID-19 pandemic, expect those same supply chains to be digitised from end to end (more on this in the next chapter).

Then there is online shopping. NBN Co (owner of the Australian high speed broadband network) told the Australian population the following.

- Almost half of the Australian population increased their online shopping during the pandemic.
- Seventy percent of us deliberately support Australian business by buying from them online.
- About the same number of us would like to support more local business but can't find what we need online because the supplier does not have a digital presence.

---

26   http://www.digitalinnovation.pwc.com.au/

Consider too what happened to cash during the pandemic. Signs appeared in most shops asking customers to use their credit or debit cards instead of cash to help contain the spread of the virus. It's rare to see cash changing hands anymore. I still feel odd paying for a $2.50 drink with Pay Wave, but I guess I'll get used to it eventually, as will we all.

Taking that thought a little further, I'm wondering if there will be other, future, implications of the almost disappearance of cash. Is there a chance that a (hopefully large) proportion of illegal activity will be stopped in a cashless society? (For that to happen, we will have to hope that Westpac, with 23 million money-laundering breaches, will learn to behave, along with its banking colleagues.)

One of the bright lights of the digital leaps forward we made in 2020 was the wide adoption of telehealth. At last, certain telehealth consultations were eligible for Medicare payments. In a country as sparsely populated as Australia, this can only be a sensible change. However, the health system, end to end, consists of silos. The pieces don't join up, even though the technology to do so has been available for some time. Here, then, is an opportunity to boost population health and economic efficiency in one project. What's not to like?

Increased digitisation does bring risks though. We are repeatedly warned about cyber security, and that increased digitisation increases the risk of occurrence.

Then there is Blockchain. I am no expert on this technology, but I know that I am going to have to get up to speed quickly – and so are you. Blockchain technology has been making gradual inroads into commerce for years. Now I believe that its time has come. Blockchain provides greater transparency and security to commercial transactions. I wrote in Chapter 5 about how when supply chains become disrupted, trust disappears. Blockchain is the technology that can rebuild that trust and remove some of the risk of dealing with unknown parties at a great distance.

This book is not the place for a lesson on how Blockchain works, but PwC estimates that by 2030, up to 20 percent of global economic commerce will run on it. Time to get the books out and start studying.

The bottom line for small business is that business models are changing, as they always do in the wake of a major disruption. Customers expect a seamless, digital commercial experience, with them at the centre.

Supply chains

Without a doubt, there will be many changes as a result of the coronavirus pandemic . And not just any old changes. Some of them will affect the way we do business every single day.

One of those changes will be how supply chains are constructed. The number-one priority of large companies is to eliminate risks in their supply chain. That's why they wouldn't buy from you if you're a small or medium sized company. You might not be able to supply consistently, or in sufficient volume. You might go broke and leave their supply chain damaged or broken.

Ironically, it is exactly that line of thinking that has created the biggest risks of all – one big company purchasing from one, or several, other big companies over a great distance, both in time and kilometres.

Supply chains will shift from being focussed on efficiency, to being focussed on reliability.

The COVID-19 pandemic shutdown response exposed the real risk. Closed factories, grounded airplanes and people, and closed borders. All of a sudden, the world was clanging like bells in the cathedral with the sound of breaking supply chains.

In the future, supply chains will shift from being focussed on efficiency, to being focussed on reliability.

As a result, those same big companies will reconfigure their supply chains to eliminate failure and/or choke points.

They will make changes such as the following.

- They will require complete transparency in their supply chains.
- They will stop relying on just one country, or one company for supply.
- They will look again at manufacturing in their own country or region.
- They will focus more on buying local.

Here lie opportunities for small and regional businesses …

Local buying/local manufacture

This will be a monumental shift, and there's a lot to consider. SME owners and managers need to be identifying possibilities now. What do you think the supply chains in your industry will look like in five years? If you say the same as now, I would suggest you haven't thought about it long enough.

The University of South Australia Director of Defence summed up the opportunity for Australian manufacturing beautifully.

> Historically Asia has won out on price but given the current situation, utilising a guaranteed supply from Australian providers should be given a higher priority over lower cost.[27]

---

27   http://australianmanufacturingnews.com/global-shutdown-could-spark-australian-manufacturing-revival/

Not only will Australia see increased demand, but regional Australia is in the box seat. In fact, this trend was already well under way when COVID-19 made its presence felt. Some of Australia's largest companies have joined the Regional Australia Institute to form the Regional Australia Council 2031. The council showcases the opportunities for investment, development and employment in regional Australia.

The opportunities for regional Australia

I'm excited about the opportunities for regional Australia in the wake of the virus disaster. Hundreds of thousands of people discovered that they don't have to live in a crowded suburb and work in a crowded inner-city office in order to be productive.

The attractions of a regional lifestyle, with the accompanying affordable housing,[28] are obvious to many. Then there's tourism. Those regular overseas trips appear to be off the menu for some time. Driving holidays to Australia's world-beating regional holiday destinations are taking their place. There are many, many regional areas that have already thought about their future.

As an example, I have previously worked with the regional Queensland Council where I live, and the state government, on projects that will build regional resilience and help to ensure our future. These projects are ready to go. They are bottom-up community projects grown out of community needs, not a "roads and bridges" project dreamed up and handed to us from on high. I don't know if our governments share my enthusiasm (or frankly, even my concern) for regional Australia, but we need to offer more than nice scenery, friendship and a short commute to attract professionals to the regions. We need to get smarter about managing perceptions.

---

28   As at February 2021, the affordable housing is becoming less affordable. Regional real estate prices have jumped an average of 7 percent as city-dwellers head for the regions.

Living in a regional area does not automatically strip someone of all education, innovation and ability.

I've noticed there is something of a gulf between city-dwellers and regional folks. One very high-profile person responded to my pitch for investment in regional areas with a comment that highlighted the misconceptions some urban folk have of areas beyond city limits. "Yes, it's very important that we support the bush," they said.

Here's the thing. Not all of regional Australia is "bush", and the comment implied that everyone in the "bush" was broke and asking for a handout.

I want to acknowledge that there are parts of regional Australia suffering from drought and the after-effects of the 2019–2020 bushfires. It's crippling to regional economies and their people, and they need support. I've lived through them with my farming family.

But even in areas where drought has a firm hand or places still in recovery from bushfire (or flood), there are innovative entrepreneurs making the world a better place.

Not 30 minutes from where I live is a world-leading agricultural robotics company called SwarmFarm.[29] Andrew and Jocie Bate are farmers who saw a better way to do agriculture using "swarmbots" instead of simply using bigger and bigger tractors, and they went for it. They collaborate with universities but insist that their company stay headquartered here, where the farming happens.

A local high-school student won a Tech Hack competition with his "Mad Greens"[30] fresh produce innovation.

Queensland's first dedicated AgTech incubator has just been established.

I have already mentioned some innovative projects being

---

29   https://www.swarmfarm.com/
30   https://www.goodfruitandvegetables.com.au/story/5725076/digbys-micro-greens-idea-snares-prize/

undertaken across Queensland, preparing our regions for a low-carbon economy.

I'm not the only person who senses this disconnect either. My colleague in charge of the AgTech incubator explained that when they were pitching the idea in Canberra, they first had to prove that they weren't dumb.

Regional Australia experiences inequality and that doesn't just affect those of us who live here; it affects everyone's wealth and wellbeing.

My plea to non-regional Australians is to start managing perceptions and look beyond sensationalist, superficial journalism. Maintain your empathy for those doing it tough anywhere, but also applaud the brilliant, adventurous, resilient entrepreneurs who reside outside the known world of capital city CBDs.

Case Study:
How BHP actively helps regional small business, and why others should follow

Way back in 2012, I attended some meetings to learn about a new program to be launched by mining giant BHP. (To be accurate, it was BMA, BHP Mitsubishi Alliance, a joint venture between BHP and Mitsubishi).

It was called the BMA Local Buying Program (now the Local Buying Program) and at its heart was a deliberate policy to engage small, local businesses as suppliers to the company's coal mines in Central Queensland.

Small, local businesses were invited to register with the program if they wished to become a supplier to the mining giant and reap the rewards of having a "big name" as a customer.

Previously, that was a step too far for many, because the paperwork and compliance bar was simply too high for them. So many forms to fill out, large insurance amounts required, too many systems to comply with ... Effectively, a small supplier of coffee cups was expected to meet the same supplier standards as a multi-million-dollar supplier of structural steel.

The attraction of the Local Buying Program was threefold.

- *The opportunity to benefit from becoming a local supplier to such a large organisation.*
- *A much simpler on-boarding process with less paperwork.*
- *Shorter payment times – less than 21 days.*

Initially, the program was met with a degree of cynicism by the small-business community – unsurprisingly, not all small-business owners trust the motives of a multinational mining company such as BHP!

As it grew, the Local Buying Program was supported by both the company and local businesses. In December 2020, the program cracked through $600 million in contract value awarded.[31] That's $600m that has been spent exclusively with small, local businesses that otherwise would most likely not have been able to participate in BHP's supply chain at all.

There is also a Give-Back piece. Apart from the direct benefit to supplying companies, there was an added attraction. For every transaction through the program, a small percentage of the contract value is deposited with an independent foundation. Under the guidance of a local advisory group, the

---

31   For updates on contract value awarded, check the website https://c-res.com.au/

foundation money is used for "building sustainable business futures" and "building sustainable business communities".

To date, just over $3.5 million has been spent by the foundation on sponsoring conferences, business workshops, programs that involve school students and much, much more. And that's just in Central Queensland.

Over time, the program expanded to BHP's operations in Mackay, and now it has spread across Australia covering all BHP, BHP Mitsubishi Alliance (BMA) and BHP Mitsui Coal (BMC) operations, and internationally to Chile.

Of course, there are detractors, but I congratulate BHP on starting this program, sticking with it through the resources downturn, and expanding it to other areas.

What would make me even happier though, would be for some of BHP's competitors and compatriots at the top end of town to follow their example and truly engage with small companies in their supply chains.

BHP has shown that the model works, and increases revenue, so there's no risk involved in following their lead. Wouldn't it be wonderful if at least 20 percent of the ASX200 listed companies started their own Local Buying Programs by the end of 2021?

Be ready for the upturn

At the end of every downturn is an upturn, but it's actually easy to miss. Go have a look back to the boom and bust graph from Chapter 1, and note the word at the bottom of the bust section: Despair.

At the bottom of the graph, that's exactly how you feel. You've been ground down by the recession (or contraction if it didn't quite meet the textbook definition of a recession). Every newspaper and news bulletin, every day, is full of gloom and doom.

The best way to describe this phase of the cycle is the old saying that "the darkest hour is just before the dawn". Just as we ignore the probability of a crash when the boom is getting towards its peak because everyone is looking at the world through rose-coloured glasses, we do the same in reverse at the bottom. (There is a psychological model to explain this, so, once again, I'm not just making this up!)

Unfortunately, I don't have an exact measure you can use (for example, the ratio of doom and gloom news stories to good stories). But just as we looked for "this time it's different" stories towards the peak of the boom, equivalent stories about why conditions won't recover will most probably appear at the low point of the crisis.

Of course, this is an extremely simplified version of a series of highly complicated events and influences, but the basic outline doesn't change.

There is one other indicator that you may like to look out for – the infamous "Lipstick Effect". When times are bad, women increase their spending on beauty products. Don't laugh – it's real! A 2012 psychology study[32] used historical data and rigorous experiments to examine why this is so. So keeping an eye on sales of beauty products may be a reliable indicator for you to follow!

32   Hill SE, Rodeheffer CD, Griskevicius V, Durante K, White AE. *Boosting beauty in an economic decline: mating, spending, and the lipstick effect.* J Pers Soc Psychol. 2012 Aug;103(2):275-91. doi: 10.1037/a0028657. Epub 2012 May 28. PMID: 22642483.

New technology will emerge

As we've seen, every downturn has an upturn. What also holds true is that every major downturn brings a technology change that has far-reaching effects.

If we look at busts throughout history, and then look a decade ahead, you will always find some of the biggest companies and brands emerged from the debris. Often, the new technology will take a long time to emerge, and even longer (typically 30 years) to become all-pervading and a common part of our lives.

There are companies that looked around, worked out that the landscape had changed, and then created products and services that suited the new environment. The most recent example is the aftermath of the 1990–1991 recession. The kings of the current stock market, – the technology companies such as Facebook, Amazon and Alphabet (Google) – all emerged out of the 1990–1991 recession and the beginnings of the internet. Along with Apple and Microsoft, these companies currently make up 50 percent of the US Technology Stock Market Index (the Nasdaq), and one-fifth of the main US Stock Index, the S&P 500. They didn't even exist 30 years ago.

Now, as a group, the tech titans Amazon, Apple, Facebook and Google are coming under increasing scrutiny over their operating methods, transparency and corporate ethics. (Incidentally, as of November 2020, the "tech barons" had accumulated an additional $565 billion in wealth since the COVID-19 pandemic started.)

Who knows what the disruptive technology emerging from the 2020 downturn will be? Something to do with climate change? Artificial intelligence? Quantum computing? Or something that we haven't even heard of yet?

We will have to wait and see, but there is another question to be answered as well. If a new technology emerges that displaces the current technology titans, those same companies that dominate the stock market, what are the implications for stock market values, and therefore us?

All we can be sure of is that some disruption will emerge, and it will dramatically change the way we do business.

The B Word. What if you don't make it?

There will be some companies that don't make it through the crisis. Unfortunately, many of them will face bankruptcy.

No doubt, some of these will carry feelings of having failed. Our society does not appreciate failure. It's unacceptable. Failure means that we're not good enough or didn't try hard enough. Failure is something to be ashamed of.

But that is just not true. Coronavirus wasn't invented by you, but it smacked you behind the head anyway. If you feel as though you have failed through this crisis, you haven't. Your failure is most probably hurt. Hurt that circumstances beyond your control have taken away opportunities.

Famous failures

Have you ever noticed how many successful entrepreneurs have a back story that includes a business failure or near-death experience?

Steve Jobs – Jobs was famously fired from Apple in 1985 before retaking the helm and creating those things that we can't seem to live our lives without now – smartphones.

Walt Disney – Yes, Walt Disney was a failure, before he practically invented American culture. He was fired from his work at a newspaper because the editor didn't think he had any good ideas or imagination.

Oprah Winfrey – She's so famous that you don't even have to say her surname. Just saying Oprah is enough. Well, she was fired from her first job at a tv station because the producer thought she was unfit for tv. I wonder if that person is still living that statement down!

Anyway, the point is that many, many people that we see as successful have failed – in some way or another – in the past. In fact, it seems to be a necessity.

If you have a few hours spare, head over to Google and read about the reasons embedded in our psychology why failure is a pre-requisite to success and, I would suggest, resilience.

So, what to do?

Your perceived failure is a chance to find out what you really want to do. In the face of perceived failure, we all have the opportunity to do one of three things.

- Retreat. Stop doing what you were doing altogether.
- Refocus on something different. Acknowledge that something went wrong with your execution, and tweak what you were doing.
- Discover that you really were on the right track. Examine your perceived failure, and whether it really was one. As one of my business mentors says, "Beware the single-person survey."

The last two alternatives involve showing up. After a stumble, you are never going to succeed unless you show up. In truth, the only time you really fail is when you don't show up and try.

If you were truly beaten up by the COVID-19 pandemic, or any other crisis in the future, take some time to think about your next steps. But please don't look upon your "failure" as a dead end. Like Oprah, Steve and Walt, it is probably just the beginning.

Chapter 6

Business Philosophy and Ethics: Looking Forward and Doing Business Better

At the end of every downturn is an upturn – at some point. Ergo, every time we have one of these crashes, we have the opportunity to re-make, rebuild, rethink, and, most of all remember, to correct our path moving forward.

I have taken the opportunity in this book to do some deeper thinking about how we can do that in the wake of the COVID-19 outbreak. The world faces some insanely difficult problems and continuing to do and act as we have always done and acted certainly won't solve them.

As the initial shock of the COVID-19 outbreak wore off, almost every commentator, including me, spoke and wrote about the possibilities before us, now that the impossible had become possible. Governments spent billions of dollars where they were previously reluctant to spend cents – on welfare, homelessness, health, childcare etc. In the words of Australia's Reserve Bank Governor Phillip Lowe, "So we're all doing things here that we thought we would never have to do."

In a series of LinkedIn and Facebook posts, I asked my social-media community: *What four things from the COVID-19 era would you like to take forward with us, and what four things would you like to leave behind?*

My community responded by citing the positive impacts of a stronger sense of community, greater action on climate change, the national cabinet model, incentivised programs on backyard gardens and single-car families and the care army among many other suggestions. There were numerous heart-warming anecdotes of bold and bright ideas. In thinking about what to leave behind, the group cited homelessness, inequality, political spin and corporate greed amongst other negative practices that I hope we all hope to put in the rear-vision mirror.

This final section of the book explores some of those difficult issues that seem intractable. I offer my thoughts on how we could approach them and make our businesses and communities, and society in general, better places to be.

I would like propose a new brand of business philosophy to tackle some of our most difficult challenges.

My image of the future revolves around the following elements:

- ethical business
- the ethics of the relationship between small and large business
- economic power and transparency in political decision-making
- resource-constrained economic growth
- valuing those who are indispensable in our lives
- environmental responsibility.

Ethical business

If you're not a business with a purpose, you're not a business making the world a better place

You've heard all the sayings "Do what you love, and you'll never work a day in your life", "Passion will make you succeed in business", and "Passion leads to success".

I have never believed that passion alone is sufficient to create a successful, growing business. You need at least nine other skills and there is now one additional ingredient that is non-negotiable.

That ingredient is purpose.

For almost 60 years, the purpose of a business was assumed to be "to make money for its shareholders". This stance was backed by mainstream economists, politicians and big business.

Milton Friedman, the economist who set off this chain of thought, told his readers that "there is one and only one social responsibility of business [which is] to use its resources and engage in activities designed to increase its profits".

But times are changing, and that attitude is changing. Purpose now refers to a strong, believable "why" that has a positive impact upon society. It is no longer sufficient to have some nice-sounding words on your boardroom wall, website and in your annual reports. Today's customers and investors have a laser-like vision and can see through that thin veneer of words.

It is also rewarding in a financial sense. Multiple investigations, academic research projects and industry surveys tell us this is so. The science is in. Organisations that have a strong, believable "why" and follow that purpose with socially responsible and sensitive actions are more likely to attract customers and suppliers.

In Chapter 4, I wrote about some companies that did not exactly act with honour during the COVID-19 pandemic. Similarly, there have been many companies that behaved badly during previous crises. Then there are those that behave badly most of the time.

Of course, there were many more that acted with empathy and responsibility. These are the companies that will be remembered by their customers, suppliers and stakeholders. These are the ones that will prosper. What today's customers, employees and investors are looking for is those organisations that truly embed social responsibility into everything they do, in every part of the organisation.

Before I go further, I'm going to decode some of the acronyms used when discussing these topics.

CSR

Corporate Social Responsibility is your responsibility, as a company, beyond your immediate economic interest. Or at a more basic level, "If I don't do some corporate philanthropy, I'll be seen as heartless and greedy."

Our thinking needs to go beyond this.

ESG

Environmental and Social Governance is how an organisation performs on three criteria.

- Environmental. Does the company operate with the least environmental disruption it can manage?
- Social. Does the company treat employees, suppliers, customers and communities with empathy and respect?
- Governance. Does the company have good internal controls, responsible leadership and respect for shareholder rights?

Your affiliation is showing

In a piece of ground-breaking research, a company in the USA[33] tracked down a strong correlation between political donations and how that company scores on ESG metrics.

Companies that donate to conservative parties in the USA (Republicans) have lower ESG scores, and companies that donate to liberal parties (Democrats) score higher. The relationship is strong, and an "exceptionally good predictor" of how companies act. In the words of one of the researchers: "These donations can tell you a lot about a company's day-to-day behaviour. And that's priceless information to have when you're deciding who to buy from or invest in."

Whether this relationship holds in countries other than the USA would be a fascinating study to undertake.

TSI

Total Societal Impact is a concept that has grown out of recent research, predominantly by the American multinational (and highly influential) management consulting firm Boston Consulting Group.[34]

Your TSI is the sum of all the ways you impact society, both positive and negative.

TSI is moving way, way beyond showing your social credentials by writing out a big cheque to your favourite charity. TSI is much broader and bigger.

---

33 https://blog.csrhub.com/do-political-donations-really-predict-corporate-behavior?utm_content=137946248&utm_medium=social&utm_source=linkedin&hss_channel=lcp-1197426

34 https://www.bcg.com/en-au/publications/2017/total-societal-impact-new-lens-strategy

Organisations embracing TSI are not just "not doing bad things" but are taking positive actions, often guided by the UN Sustainable Development Goals. They incorporate social and environmental considerations into everything they do.

And it seems that those at the very top end of the business tree are coming to believe this as well. In 2019, 180 leaders of some of the biggest corporations in existence put their names to a document called "A Statement on the Purpose of a Corporation". The statement declared that profits for shareholders is no longer the most important task of companies.

There are some heavy hitters in this group. The CEOs of Amazon, American Airlines, JP Morgan Chase, and even Lachlan Murdoch then CEO of Fox Corporation all signed.

The document states:

> While each of our individual companies serves its own corporate purpose, we share a fundamental commitment to all of our stakeholders … We commit to deliver value to all of them, for the future success of our companies, our communities and our country.

That sounds liked a very sensible statement. We would like to think that our biggest companies have a commitment to the wellbeing of their employees, customers, suppliers, and society as a whole. But have they put their money where their mouth is? Subsequent research showed that of the original signatories, only two checked with their board before endorsing such a major change. The implication is that they didn't really expect to make any major changes at all, and therefore did not bother to seek board approval.[35]

---

35 Was the Business Roundtable Statement on Corporate Purpose Mostly for Show? – (1) Evidence from Lack of Board Approval, https://corpgov.law.harvard.edu/2020/08/12/was-the-business-roundtable-statement-on-corporate-purpose-mostly-for-show-1-evidence-from-lack-of-board-approval/

Why you should be genuine about your social responsibility

There are several excellent reasons why you should be joining the growing number of socially responsible organisations – the ones that question how their work makes the world a better place.

It's the right thing to do

Firstly, of course, because it's the right thing to do. I don't have to expand on this one.

Global investment markets are watching you

Global money is increasingly filtering where investment funds are allocated by looking at social purpose. The amount of money involved in this "impact investing" is currently $502 billion (yes, with a 'b'), and growing. That's one-quarter of all global assets under management.

Firms controlling almost $US90 trillion in global assets have signed on to a United Nations–backed Principles for Responsible Investment pledge to disclose climate risk and other ESG considerations.[36]

The conclusion to be drawn from these figures is that if your organisation wants to be considered by global fund managers and investors, you will have to be one of your industry's leaders in social responsibility.

I know that there is still a sector of investors that push for short-term financial results, but there is that growing wave of capital that is looking more long term. You already know that your customers and potential investors can take to social media at a moment's notice and trash your corporate reputation in an instant.

---

36   https://www.theaustralian.com.au/business/the-deal-magazine/ethical-investment-global-scorecard/news-story/83ab423b8fc9dcc7d29224e31c1202a0

Your shareholders are watching you

Apart from the acronyms I introduced earlier in this section, two measures that you and your shareholders will already understand are Total Company Valuation, and profit margins. These influence that all-important financial metric that you also know, Total Shareholder Return (TSR).

The Boston Consulting Group research I mentioned earlier examined four industries and identified the things that customers and investors expect companies in that industry to do to get top marks on CSR/TSI.

- In the Oil and Gas industry, high TSI companies had a 19 percent valuation premium, and a 3.4 percent margin premium over the industry average.

- In packaged consumer goods, the figures were 11 percent valuation premium and 4.8 percent margin premium.

Wouldn't it be a nice feeling to see your total company valuation increase by 19 percent, and your margins by 4–5 percent or more? And your shareholders would also share that feeling.

Your employees are watching you

Your employees have lost trust in the major institutions that dominate our societies. The Edelman Trust Barometer Report tell us that sixty-five percent of informed people and 47 percent of the mass population distrust institutions. These people are disenchanted and feel the frustration of not being able to create positive changes in their world through the traditional institutions, including politicians.

People are turning to their employers to help them navigate a world that is letting them down. Seventy-five percent of people surveyed in the latest Edelman Trust Barometer say they trust their employer. That's 27 points more than government.

The global consulting firm McKinsey also tells us that:

In a recent McKinsey survey of US workers, 82 percent of the more than 1,000 respondents affirmed the importance of corporate purpose, but only 42 percent reported that their company's stated purpose had much effect. This is a cautionary tale about the generic nature of most companies' statements on identity but also the identification of an opportunity to surprise and sway skeptical stakeholders.[37]

So if you want to attract the best, brightest and most committed employees to your team, you will have to meet their expectations of being a leader on social action.

You need to attract the best and brightest employees. We old ones are wearing out, so you have to look to the millennials. This lot have a real social conscience. Three quarters of them say they would take a pay cut to work for a responsible company. Almost nine out of 10 say that their jobs are more fulfilling if they have opportunities in their work role to make a positive impact. You need these people, and they won't stay with you if your concept of CSR stops at writing some nice policies to put on the office walls.

Your customers are watching you

Consumers are increasingly voting with their dollars and shun companies that do not align with their values and desire to make the world a better place. More than eighty percent of consumers expect that their purchases will give them more than just a product or service. Three out of four consumers will purchase "responsible" brands.

I found a quote recently that sums up this trend beautifully.

---

37   https://www.mckinsey.com/business-functions/organization/our-insights/demonstrating-corporate-purpose-in-the-time-of-coronavirus

"An increasing number of people recognise that their money should do more than just make more money."[38]

Research by global bank HSBC showed that organisations with ESG good practice held their value better as stock markets crashed on COVID-19 uncertainly.[39]

> Our core ESG conviction is that issuers succeed long-term, and hence deliver shareholder returns when they create value for all stakeholders – employees, customers, suppliers, the environment, and wider society. When crises like COVID-19 manifest, particularly with social and environmental causes and implications, investors can see ESG as a defensive characteristic.

Social responsibility and small business

There are many responsibilities that you carry as a small-business owner. Your responsibility to make a positive social impact is right up there with the traditional roles.

So now that you've considered the reasons why joining the growing number of socially responsible organisations is important, what are you currently doing and how can you continue to ensure that your small business is helping to make the world a better place? How do you go about this?

The answers aren't easy. So here's a challenge. What is your role in your company's Total Societal Impact? Is your company going to be on the front foot, or dragging the chain? Believe me, some of your competitors are already onto it.

---

38   Unfortunately I didn't note down where I got the quote from, so if it was you, and you are reading this book, please let me know so I can give you the correct attribution!

39   https://www.gbm.hsbc.com/insights/global-research/esg-stocks-did-best-in-corona-slump

Communicating the importance of social responsibility, not financials

The first step involves communication and recognising that finance people and environment, social and governance people speak different languages. Each needs to understand the importance of the other. You, as the busines owner or manager, are in charge of the communication messages that come from your company. You are the ones who communicate your financial results to your investors and the world, so it's your responsibility to put equal weight on your TSI/CSR/ESG reporting. If you talk about financial results all the time, don't be surprised if that's all that others concentrate on. Your teams need to be bi-lingual.

Business ethics, or how you behave when nobody is looking

Related to, but not exactly the same as TSI and Social Licence, is the topic of corporate ethics or how you behave when no-one is looking.

This is another issue that has found its way from the fringe press to the mainstream, particularly courtesy of the Royal Commission into Misconduct in the Banking, Superannuation and Financial Services Industry (Banking Royal Commission) 2017–2019. Pick up any copy of the *Australian Financial Review*, *Financial Times*, *New York Times* or other quality newspaper, and you will almost inevitably see a story about business ethics, director's responsibilities or a tale of corporate malfeasance.

Believe it or not, ethics will be a critical success factor for business into the future.

I have already discussed unethical behaviour. In Chapter 4, I detailed how customers are watching you during a crisis. Earlier in this chapter, I highlighted how important it is to have a purpose in your business beyond making money.

The banking and finance oath

I also mentioned the Banking Royal Commission in the second paragraph of this chapter. There is no clearer illustration of how corporate ethics became warped in the pursuit of profit, how fine-sounding statements meant nothing, and how appalling behaviour became normalised because "everyone was doing it", than this unedifying display of corporate hubris.

What added insult to injury was that the industry regulators, charged with keeping the industry honest, were negligent as well. In the words of the commissioner, "When misconduct was revealed, it either went unpunished or the consequences did not meet the seriousness of what had been done." Then there is the matter of our political leaders doing everything they could to stop the inquiry happening in the first place.

I thoroughly recommend the book *Banking Bad* by Adele Ferguson. Adele was the journalist who broke the stories that led to the royal commission. I purchased the audiobook version and listened to it on one of my regular long road trips. I found myself in tears several times, listening to the heartbreaking stories of lives and businesses ruined by unconscionable decisions emanating from our major financial institutions.

The Banking and Finance Oath illustrates just how far apart rhetoric and fact had moved. In 2013, the Banking and Finance Oath was launched.

The oath asserts the ethical and moral foundation of the finance industry.

The vision: A banking and finance industry that meets the community's needs and has its full confidence thereby fulfilling its integral role in society.

Trust is the foundation of my profession.

- I will serve all interests in good faith.
- I will compete with honour.
- I will pursue my ends with ethical restraint.
- I will help create a sustainable future.
- I will help create a more just society.
- I will speak out against wrongdoing and support others who do the same.
- I will accept responsibility for my actions.

In these and all other matters, my word is my bond.

That didn't turn out so well …

What can we get away with?

It appears to me, and to many others, that the guiding ethical principle for too many organisations is not "what is the right thing to do", but "what can we get away with"?

There are many examples, and I'm sure you get the idea, but indulge me while I list a few instances that illustrate the point, but that you may have missed.

- In 2020, mining giant Rio Tinto destroyed a 46,000-year-old cultural heritage site at Juukan Gorge in Western Australia to expand a minesite. Yes, the action was legal, but legal and ethical aren't always the same thing.
- Sexual harassment cases that still occur and are not dealt with adequately.
- Australia's horror 2020 bushfire season. While not ultimately preventable, there is no doubt that ignoring repeated warnings constitutes an ethical failure.
- Withholding executive bonuses as "punishment" for unethical behaviour. The underlying message being reinforced is that money is pre-eminent. Foregoing dollars absolves unethical behaviour.

- The COVID 19 pandemic during 2020 produced some note-worthy examples:
  - o Several Australian companies paid increased dividends and bonuses when Government stimulus packages (JobKeeper) were issued to help keep employees on the books.
  - o British entrepreneur and founder of Virgin airlines Richard Branson requested UK taxpayer assistance, despite not having paid tax in the UK for 14 years.
  - o US lawmakers requested five large corporations return their share of $50 million that was meant for small businesses. Apparently, only one returned the money.[40]

Ethics moments

It's one thing to point out ethical failure in business, so in the spirit of "don't bring me problems; bring me solutions", I have a proposal that will help eliminate them.

One of my volunteer positions is as a member of the Queensland Workplace Health and Safety Expert Reference Group. I'm certainly not an expert on safety, but I brought a knowledge of small business to the group. For SME owners, one of the perceived barriers to working with a big company is the safety standards that these organisations require of their suppliers.

Note that I said "perceived" barriers. There actually is a disconnect here between the beliefs of the small-business owner and the big company. Both sides of the transaction are looking at the same problem, but from different points of view. One believes that the systems are too hard and costly to implement, while the other believes that small businesses can't be suppliers because their systems just aren't good enough.

The disconnect creates a barrier to potentially successful

---

40   https://www.businessinsider.com.au/us-representatives-blast-large-companies-small-business-coronavirus-loans-2020-5

commercial relationships, and it dawned on me that the same disconnect exists on the matter of corporate ethics.

While big businesses don't believe that small suppliers can live up to their safety expectations, small businesses often don't believe that they will be treated fairly by their big customers.

Another disconnect.

Safety moments vs ethics moments

One of the simplest ways to raise awareness of safety in the workplace is the use of "safety moments", where teams or individuals simply stop, assess and think about the task they are about to perform. So, if safety moments are successful in raising awareness of safety and safety outcomes, why don't we have "ethics moments" as well?

It would be very simple, and only take a little bit of time.

Just stop and think about the task or act you are about to perform and ask yourself, "Is this really the right thing to do?"

If we apply the reasoning behind safety moments and embrace the concept of ethics moments, we may just promote an environment where ethical behaviour is the norm.

The ethical dimension of business relationships: small business versus big business

Two big ethical issues plague the relationship between small business and big business: getting paid and unfair contracts.

Payment terms

Who thinks small businesses should get the $7 billion they are entitled to? That is what it's costing small business owners every year because their big customers don't pay on time.

The popular small business financial software platform Xero did a study of payments. They found that 53 percent of payments to small businesses are late. That totals $215 billion every year being late, or $52,000 for every small business in the country.

Importantly, they also calculated that paying on time would save small business. That's where the $7 billion figure comes in.

Extended payment terms. This is when a large company has a policy that it doesn't pay its suppliers for longer than what would be considered normal trading terms, that is 14 or 30 days. There's been a gradual creep from 30 days up to 45, 60, 90, or even 120 days. In fact a research report published in the early 2000s uncovered 365-day payment terms!

Late payments. This is when the payment isn't made until after the due date. That due date maybe 120 days from invoice, so if the invoice isn't paid on time you can see how that just compounds the problem.

Reverse factoring or supply chain finance. This is where the large company tells the supplier that they can get paid early, such as at 30 days, but only if they discount their invoice.

For late payments, Australia is the world record holder, but it's not something that we should be proud of though. On average, Australian companies pay 26.4 days late[41] and that's on top of the long trading terms of 45, 60, 90, or even 120 days. And all research shows that the worst payers of all are big companies. No doubt, more recent research will emerge and show that figure increased during the COVID-19 pandemic. As an example, Supercheap Auto moved from 60 day to 90-day terms. And that's not from the date of invoice. That's from the first of the month AFTER a correct invoice was received.

Reverse factoring also featured during the coronavirus crisis but with a twist. A small supplier was already giving a 3 percent discount to the large customer to get paid in 30 days. (Even that

---

41   https://www.asbfeo.gov.au/inquiries/payment-times-and-practices

part is wrong.) Just before payment day, the big customer contacted the supplier and invited them to tender for how big a discount they would offer in order to get paid. The hint was that most suppliers were tendering in the region of 15–20 percent discount. That would wipe out small businesses' margins, at least, and probably eat into their capital as well.

The arguments about payment terms have been going on for years as you can see from the timeline below. There have been incremental concessions by government and big business, slow and painful, and mostly useless.

A brief history of Payment Times Regulation in Australia

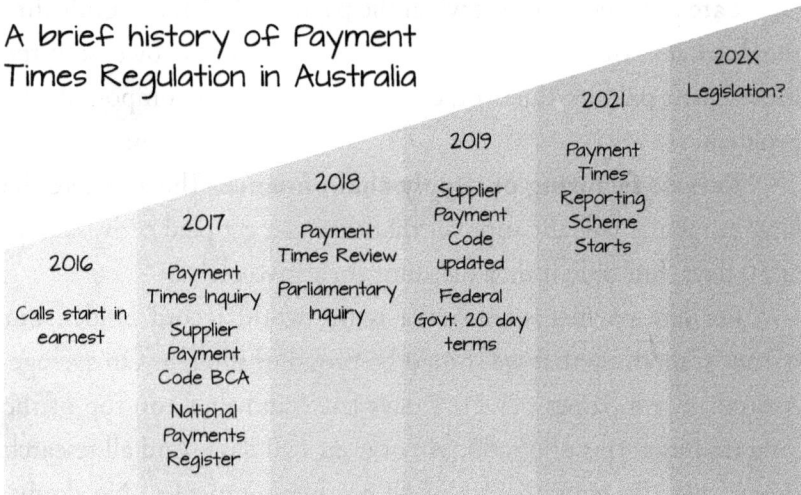

2016	2017	2018	2019	2021	202X
Calls start in earnest	Payment Times Inquiry	Payment Times Review	Supplier Payment Code updated	Payment Times Reporting Scheme Starts	Legislation?
	Supplier Payment Code BCA	Parliamentary Inquiry	Federal Govt. 20 day terms		
	National Payments Register				

The latest iteration is the Payment Times Reporting Scheme (started on 1 January 2021). Under this scheme, large businesses and large government enterprises have to publicly report their small business payment terms and times.

Some research a few years ago[42] allowed us to drill down to regional effects of late payments. When the mining boom turned to mining bust in 2012–2013, most of the large mining companies

---

42   https://www.resourceindustrynetwork.org.au/Portals/13/Economic%20
      Analysis%20of%20Impacts%20of%20Extended%20Payment%20Terms%20
      Report%20by%20Lytton%20Advisory.pdf

stretched their payment terms out to 60–90 days. This was done to protect their own cash reserves. An industry organisation in the Bowen Basin mining area of Queensland conducted research to quantify exactly how much these late payments were costing the region. The research found that if payment terms were uniformly 30 days, that simple action would create an additional:

- 380 jobs over five years,
- $150 million extra in wages, and
- $250 million extra of gross regional product.

I don't know about you, but that seems like a decent economic boost to me.

And it's not just dollars. The Xero study showed that small businesses that consistently receive their payments late grow at a slower rate than average. In fact they grow their revenue about a third slower than those businesses that get paid on time or before time.

We all know that economists and politicians obsess about our national productivity. Small-business owners spend 12 days a year chasing invoices that aren't paid, instead of contributing to the economy by producing and selling goods and services. This forces the business owner to focus on surviving rather than thriving.

Which leads to the next point: the stress and mental-health effects. Just over half of Australia's small-business owners say that late payments are a significant cause of panic attacks, anxiety, stress and depression. Some cite site suicidal feelings and experience emotions of extreme anger.

What price do we put on that?

Post COVID-19, I believe there is a perfect opportunity, and the perfect reason, to introduce legislation. Maximum 30-day payment terms is the solution. Twenty days would be better.

Unfair contracts

Another topic that also causes a great deal of angst amongst small-business owners is unfair contract terms. In summary, unfair contract terms exist when one party to a contract has significantly more rights than the other.

Currently, unfair contract terms are ostensibly controlled in Australia. Where a (usually large) organisation offers a contract to a (usually smaller) supplier on a "take it or leave it" basis, the supplier can apply to the courts if they believe some of the terms are unfair. The courts can declare the terms to be unfair, and therefore void.

Therein lies the problem. The supplier is the one who has to take action. The probability of a small business owner having (a) the money, (b) the time, or (c) the intestinal fortitude to refer a huge customer to the ACCC is, I would suggest, fairly low. This was always a problem with the unfair contracts legislation.

In November 2020, the commonwealth and state and territory governments agreed to strengthen these existing unfair contract term protections by making unfair terms unlawful and giving courts the power to impose a civil penalty. This is a huge step forward, but we need to see the legislation first before getting too excited. Hopefully the legislation will recognise, at last, that the relationship between a small company and a very large one is not a "normal" business-to-business relationship.

Earlier I proposed that we incorporate ethics moments into our daily business routines. My plea to large organisations is to make these two issues first on your ethics moments list in the post-pandemic business world.

Economic power

I have already spoken about business ethics and social purpose. This section will touch on a related subject – the exercise of economic power. I am definitely noticing an increase in content on the topic of political and economic power in Australia, and who wields it.

And it's not small business holding the upper hand.

Who is wielding the power?

This is a topic that I have often pondered, particularly as a regional-business owner. So many decisions that have an immense impact upon our regional economies are made a long, long way from here. These decisions are made with very little or zero input from those of us who will be affected.

When I broach the topic with those in elevated positions, I'm often told "that's just the way it is", or "that's just the way the economy works". I have asked directors of multi-national mining companies and senior public servants how the resources boom and bust was handled so badly, given that those organisations have floors and floors of economists and planners at their beck and call. The response was always a variation on the theme of "markets always overshoot. We just get over-enthusiastic at times".

I've never felt that this is a satisfactory response, and it seems there are others who agree.

In 2018, I discovered a book titled *Game Of Mates: How Economic Favours Bleed The Nation*. In the book, authors Cameron Murray and Paul Frijters tell "a tale of economic theft across major sectors of Australia's economy". The prototypical villain James, and his mates are at the top of the economic tree. And they act to deprive Bruce, the average Aussie, of his fair share of the economic pie. They act to deprive him through lobbying and generally assuring that the rules of the game favour their ilk.

The ABC has previously run a series of podcasts on the theme of "Who runs this place". Not surprisingly, the series reveals the amount of power that James and his colleagues wield, and just how they wield it.

Under Australian law, lobbyists have to be registered. Of the almost 500 lobbyists so registered, some 40 percent are "former government officials". Apparently, this number is on the rise.

But that's not the end of the story. Industry bodies that clearly influence governments are not considered to be lobbyists and are therefore exempt from any scrutiny under the appropriate codes of conduct. Include in this group Trade Unions, the Minerals Council of Australia, the Property Council of Australia, and the Pharmacy Guild.

Lobbyists only have to declare their "former government representative" past if they were a federal government minister, or a ministerial staffer, parliamentary secretary, public servant or defence-force member.

Consequently, there are many former state politicians (including state premiers or ministers), state political staffers, federal opposition or backbench staffers who have gone on to make profitable, and influential, careers as lobbyists.

My question to politicians

I wrote a post after the 2019 Federal Budget was released expressing concern that the Treasurer, Josh Frydenberg's cheer squad for the budget speech consisted of some business associates. These associates had a combined net worth of over $9billion.

My post read:

I read in this morning's papers that Josh had his own personal cheer squad along to hear his speech and join the after party. I have no problem with Josh inviting his friends to witness a major speech. That would be churlish. I'm just a bit concerned that his friendship group consists of business mates with a combined net worth of over AUD$9 billion.

Even that is ok. Everyone has the right to choose their friends. But I wonder if there are any more common (as in there are more of them) Australians around to chat in his ear? How do I get an invite to one of those after parties so I can give Josh a bit of advice from the other end of the business spectrum?

So who is wielding the political and economic power in Australia?

My question remains.

How do we change the status quo, and how does small business get a "seat at the table". If *Game of Mates* and the ABC's *Who Runs This Place?* are correct, we are still vastly outnumbered.

Growth isn't the only paradigm. Doughnut economics, collapse and the precipice

The "growth" paradigm is one of those things that we simply accept. Economic growth is good. Recall the 2019 Australian Federal election. I swore that if I heard "jobs and growth" one more time I would blow a fuse. We have organised our entire societies and economies around the fact that the number-one task of governments is to produce economic growth.

"We have organised our entire societies and economies around the fact that the number one task of governments is to produce economic growth."

That assumption (that growth is good, and necessary) makes an additional assumption – that there are unlimited physical resources that will allow that growth to continue. But what if that assumption is not true? Apart from the challenge of climate collapse – more on that later – we must seriously question whether there really is enough land, water, soil, minerals etc. to permit unending economic growth.

Economist Kate Raworth tackled this conundrum in her 2017 bestselling book *Doughnut Economics: Seven Ways to Think Like a 21st-Century Economist.*

Raworth sees the global economy as a doughnut. The "dough" part is the state where everyone has their needs met without damage to the planet. The "hole" of the doughnut is where people do not have access to the essentials of life – clean water, sanitation, health-care, equity, education etc. The doughnut's outer edge is the limit of the planet's resources. When we push beyond this limit, we are pushing too far – the ecological ceiling. Beyond this limit, we are damaging the planet's biodiversity, water, soil, oceans and so on.

Evidence that this is happening is not hard to come by. We humans have wiped out 60 percent of animal populations since 1970.[43] Australia has managed to send 100 species into extinction since European settlement.[44] Over 2 billion hectares of previously productive land has been degraded to the point of not being able to sustain production.[45] More recently, there is the legacy of the 2019–2020 Australian bushfires.

Our goal, then, should be to maintain our economic activity in the doughnut area by meeting the basic needs of all humanity, within the planet's capacity.

"All good in theory," I hear you say, "but it's not practical." On the contrary, Doughnut Economics is being embraced by main-stream economists and it is popping up in the general news media more and more often. In fact, the city of Amsterdam has adopted

43   https://www.theguardian.com/environment/2018/oct/30/humanity-wiped-out-animals-since-1970-major-report-finds

44   https://theconversation.com/scientists-re-counted-australias-extinct-species-and-the-result-is-devastating-127611

45   http://www.fao.org/news/story/en/item/1294000/icode/

Doughnut Economics as its framework for rebuilding after the coronavirus pandemic.

According to the city's Deputy Mayor, "It is to help us to not fall back on easy mechanisms … The doughnut does not bring us the answers but a way of looking at it, so that we don't keep on going on in the same structures as we used to."

Of course, accepting Doughnut Economics as a model implies that we move away from focussing on Gross Domestic Product (GDP) as a measure of economic growth and success. Many clever people have already thought about this and come up with several alternatives.[46] These measures attempt to incorporate quality of life, wellbeing and happiness. Some concentrate on wealth – a kind of balance sheet approach in place of the profit and loss bent of GDP. In fact, some countries have already started the process of moving away from GDP as the be-all and end-all of economic goals. Our near-neighbour, New Zealand, has adopted one of those alternatives, the "Happiness Index". Iceland and Greenland are heading down the same path.

Can the rest of us take Amsterdam's lead and take a new look at economic growth? Yes, planning will be required, as will a change in thinking – certainly by our leaders – but surely that is not impossible?

Some of us have started already.

One example is about an ongoing project in my home region (the Central Highlands of Queensland) – the Clean Growth Choices project.

In 2019, the Queensland Government implemented a Communities in Transition program, to prepare our state for a low-carbon future.

A number of local governments throughout the state joined in, and we asked ourselves whether our community is prepared to take

---

46   Coyle D, GDP needs an upgrade. Here's why, World Economic Forum, Feb 2019
      https://www.weforum.org/agenda/2019/02/what-will-succeed-gdp/

advantage of the opportunities and manage the risks of change. Do we accept that our future quality of life is determined locally as part of the community, and not waiting for the "next big thing" to be handed to us from on high?

Our region settled on three pathways to follow in order to strengthen our resilience.

- Circular economy, including agricultural technology.
- Supply chains – how our supply chains connect with the world.
- Building human capacity and social capital.

It was during the discussions leading to these decisions that some magic started. As the conversation about projects developed, participants began sharing commercial in confidence information. They could see the bigger picture, and how the various sectors and projects could fit together to make a greater whole. Now, the projects chosen by our region are under way, as are projects in the other participating regions.

Income and Wealth Inequality

This topic could also be the subject of its own book. In fact, it is the subject of many books, by authors who have studied the subject in depth and know much more than I. But it is such an important topic that I must include it in this "hopeful" section of my book.

Along with corporate ethics, business purpose, and corporate social responsibility, income and wealth inequality has also begun to appear in the mainstream media as opposed to fringe, academic and specialist publications.

Income and wealth inequality refers to the fact that a small number of people own a vastly disproportionate amount of the world's income and wealth. There is an abundance of shocking statistics available on the internet to illustrate. Here are just a few from a report by UK-based charity organisation Oxfam, released at the end of 2019.[47]

- The world's 2,153 billionaires have more wealth than the 4.6 billion people who make up 60 percent of the planet's population.
- The 22 richest men in the world have more wealth than all the women in Africa.
- Women and girls put in [a combined] 12.5 billion hours of unpaid care work each and every day. This contributes at least $10.8 trillion a year to the global economy, a figure more than three times the size of the global tech industry.
- Getting the richest one percent to pay just 0.5 percent extra tax on their wealth over the next 10 years would equal the investment needed to create 117 million jobs in sectors such as elderly and childcare, education and health.

Here in Australia, the top 10 percent own 50 percent of the wealth, and the top 1 percent own just over 16 percent. Those who are clustered at the top of the wealth tree will always point to their superior business and investing skills, and/or their age (the longer you live, the more time you have to accumulate assets).

But all their activity takes place within a framework of government policy and legislation, and that has enormous power to change inequality:

- investment policy
- taxation policy

---

47   https://www.oxfam.org/en/press-releases/worlds-billionaires-have-more-wealth-46-billion-people

- housing policy
- development policy
- gender policy
- health policy
- education policy, and so on.

Every election, we hear prospective governments promising to improve health and education. Ironically, it is these two aspects of society that are most adversely affected by inequality. The poor suffer from worse health and have worse education outcomes. Clearly, these have the effect of dragging down the economy as a whole.

The COVID-19 pandemic was a graphic illustration of what inequality in society does. Different social groups were impacted differently – sometimes vastly so. The poor carried by far the worst impacts of coronavirus. Health outcomes for lower socio-economic cohorts were worse.

- Isolating at home was impossible for the homeless.
- Studying at home was impossible for those without access to technology.
- The majority of jobs lost were those in low-paid occupations.
- Women (who earn less than men) were disproportionately impacted.

In the extreme, fractures appear in social stability. It is no coincidence that social unrest erupted in the USA and several other countries during the pandemic.

Meanwhile, the Swiss multinational bank UBS reported that the collective wealth of the world's billionaires increased by more than 27 percent during the pandemic. The tech billionaires did particularly well, from the rest of us conducting our lives via the internet and watching endless repeats on Netflix! We all raced to using internet platforms during the coronavirus pandemic. All our meetings were via Zoom, Skype and their competitors. Millions of us tuned out of the real world and into Nexflix, Stan and the other streaming entertainment channels.

The fact that the topic of inequality has also made its way into the mainstream press, alongside business ethics and social responsibility, is no surprise at all, indicating that action is nigh after decades of talkfests.

The share of income going to the 1% richest households has nearly tripled in the last four decades

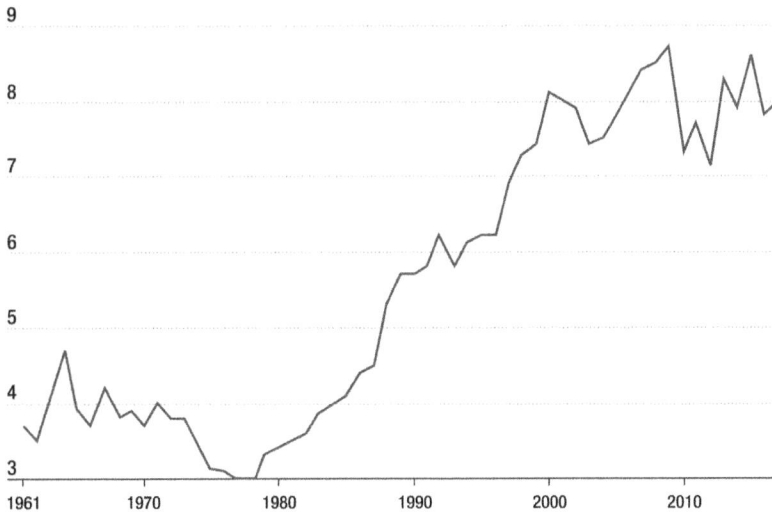

Guardian graphic. Source: IFS Deaton Review analysis of the Family Expenditure Survey and Family Resources Survey, various years.[48]

Whom do we value? Gender Inequality

This is another topic that has started to make its way into the mainstream newspapers – particularly after the COVID-19

---

48   https://www.theguardian.com/news/2019/sep/09/inequality-is-it-rising-and-can-we-reverse-it

pandemic – but it did get a good run after the 2008 Global Financial Crisis hit. Banks were bailed out, but regular companies were left to their own devices, creating a privileged class of those considered worthy of "saving".

In times such as those, it's really, really hard to remain confident that attitudes can be changed in our society. It is widely acknowledged that the social and economic effects of the COVID-19 pandemic and shutdowns hit women harder than men. Depressingly, the International Monetary Fund estimates that 30 years of gains for women in the world of work could be erased in the aftermath of the pandemic. If the experience of relying on women-dominated professions, and women in general, to survive the pandemic was not enough to make a change, what will? Nurses, teachers, mums (not exclusively but mostly) doing home schooling …

It smells of "we really need you and the economy needs you, but we don't want to pay you, because we don't think you're that important."

Environmental Responsibility and Climate Change

I personally prefer the terms "climate collapse" or "ecosystem collapse". I believe they better describe what is happening in our world.

At the end of January 2020, I fulfilled a 30-year dream to visit Antarctica.[49] It was life-changing. Of course I was prepared to be stunned and amazed by the beauty of the place but what I wasn't prepared for was the ravages of climate change that was really confronting as it's happening three times faster down there and the effects are obvious. Penguins are making their nests in the wrong

---

49   You can check out some of my photos at my website bronwynreid.com.au

place and then the chicks drown. While we were there, the continent recorded its highest ever temperature of 18.3 degrees.

I wrote in Chapter 3 about the importance of keeping on top of changes happening in your external environment – your PESTLE analysis. I contend that the effects of climate change impact on every single one of those elements. To bury one's head in the sand and not take it into account in your business planning is simply negligent. Already, company directors world-wide are waking up to the possibility of legal action over their inaction on climate change. Here in Australia, our laws governing companies require directors to act in the best interests of their company.

Australia isn't a world leader on much to do with climate change, but we did manage to have the world's first legal action over whether investment managers were taking it into consideration in their investment decisions.[50] The plaintiff, 23-year-old Mark McVeigh alleged that the trustees of his superannuation (retirement) fund were failing to protect him from losses due to the financial impacts of climate change. The superannuation fund eventually reached a settlement with McVeigh.[51]

But Australia has had not just one legal first, but two. A group of Torres Strait Islanders took the world's first human rights complaint to the United Nations in May 2019. The complaint alleges that the Australian Government is "breaching their fundamental rights to culture and life by failing to adequately address climate change".

According to the group, sea level rise has inundated their traditional burial grounds and is washing away their homes and infrastructure.[52]

50   https://www.abc.net.au/news/2020-01-18/mark-mcveigh-is-taking-on-rest-super-and-has-the-world-watching/11876360

51   You can read the full text of the Fund's statement at https://rest.com.au/why-rest/about-rest/news/rest-reaches-settlement-with-mark-mcveigh

52   As at December 2020, the complaint was still being considered by the United Nations Human Rights Committee.

More legal challenges have commenced in Australia and internationally, and no doubt more will follow as the novel subject of climate change becomes a common thread in commercial law.

Nature's shots over the bow

Nature has given us several shots over the bow to warn of the risks of ignoring climate change. We've seen bushfires, wild floods, tornadoes, glacier melts, and those effects that I witnessed in Antarctica. COVID-19 may just be the warning shot about the supply chain interruptions we can expect from increasingly violent and frequent weather events.

As we saw in 2020 and beyond, supply chains had been set up to extract maximum efficiency, not resilience. When the aeroplanes and people stopped, supply chains broke. Now, consider how much that we depend upon will be interrupted if hurricanes increase in severity. So much of what we (and the rest of the world) import comes from China and the Western Pacific. The probability of a one in 100-year hurricane hitting this area may double or quadruple by 2040.[53]

We can expect more warnings from nature in the coming years.

---

53   https://www.mckinsey.com/business-functions/sustainability/our-insights/confronting-climate-risk

A Challenge For You

Thank you for reading my book. It carries quite a bit of my heart and soul, as well as some of the time-consuming and expensive business lessons I have learned.

At the time of writing, the COVID-19 pandemic drags on, and we don't know exactly what is ahead of us. We all hope that the scientists working on vaccines and treatments are successful. I also hope that this pandemic has taught us to value those who do so much to make our societies work, but are consistently either ignored or undervalued. The doctors, nurses, scientists, teachers, carers, waste-collection teams, sewage treatment workers ... You get the idea. The people who aren't featured in newspapers and magazines.

Now I have a challenge for you.

Actually put the recommendations in this book into action. Download the resources and extra material from my website, get your team together, and start creating your Risk Management Plan. I would love it if you shared your plan with me. Of course, I don't want to know all your company secrets, but I am eternally curious about what hazards are developing out there that I am not seeing.

Incorporate my tips from Chapters 3, 4 and 5 into your Risk Management Plan, using them as strategies to reduce both the likelihood and the impact of any hazardous events that may come your way.

Your Risk Management Plan can double as your Crisis Recovery Plan as you look forward to the upturn. By thinking through the consequences of the events that might happen to you early, you are also on your way to recovery. Remember the research I referred to earlier about UK companies that had done some serious thinking about the consequences of Brexit? Those companies are doing better than their compatriots. They have adapted to the new normal and are at the front of the curve for that inevitable recovery. You will be in the best possible position to spot opportunities and be at the front of the recovery curve if you have planned and thought about potential crises before they happen.

Lastly, I sincerely hope that your future plans will include some of my hopeful suggestions for doing business better and contributing to solving some of humanity's fiendishly difficult problems. Doing so is just good business sense.

I hope that you have absorbed some knowledge from this book that will help you build a purpose-driven, resilient business that makes a difference for you, your family, and the community around you.

Me? I'm waiting until it's safe to take a return trip to Antarctica. See you there!

Acknowledgements

To Ann Wilson and Dixie Carlton of IndieExperts, my publishers – thank you. Somehow, you have managed to turn the hundreds of scrambled ideas swirling in my head into a coherent and structured book.

To Andrew Griffiths – world champion mentor and person who will always give an honest appraisal of my work. I, along with many others, am so fortunate to have encountered you along my business journey. All of us are all much better practitioners, and people, because of it.

To my family, especially the world's best husband, Ian. Thank you for supporting me once again through getting a book done. Sala – this book is half yours. Thank you for all your input, suggestions, and general counselling when I was close to becoming a blithering wreck.

To the 4T Team. Thank you for taking the load while I wrote this. Kelle and Tracey – you rock.

To those who attended my last book launch – there will not be a repeat.

Lastly, a thank you to everyone who had a part in supporting me to write this book, and then in producing it. It takes a village.

IS THAT ALL?

I know you have enjoyed reading my book – otherwise you wouldn't have made it to the end. But our friendship doesn't have to stop now, just because you've read these 100+ pages! I'd love to see us stay connected and there are easy ways for us to do that.

You can head to my website for my latest thoughts, helpful resources, information about training, and other products at:

bronwynreid.com.au

Otherwise, you can connect with me on the following social media platforms:

LinkedIn @bronwyn_reid
Facebook @smallcompanybigbusiness
Instagram @bronwyn_reid
Twitter @bronwyn_reid
YouTube @bronwynreid
Clubhouse @bronwyn_reid

Chances are that by the time you read this book, some social media platforms will have disappeared and new ones (maybe ones we haven't even thought of yet!) will have taken their place; so, I'll undertake to update this book when the time seems right. You can follow my Amazon author page to be notified of any updates and new books I publish, at:

https://amzn.to/31Vonp0

Training and mentoring.

Did you know that Bronwyn Reid is available to work one-to-one with small to medium businesses? You can engage Bronwyn for a range of services that will enable your business to thrive long before crisis hits – and maybe even serve on a future rescue team rather than needing to be rescued yourself!

www.ingramcontent.com/pod-product-compliance
Lightning Source LLC
Chambersburg PA
CBHW071705210326
41597CB00017B/2336